LINES IN THE SAND

LINES IN THE SAND

Justice and the Gulf War

Alan Geyer
and
Barbara G. Green

Westminster/John Knox Press
Louisville, Kentucky

Book design by Gene Harris

First edition

Published by Westminster/John Knox Press
Louisville, Kentucky

This book is printed on acid-free paper that meets the American National Standards Institute Z39.48 standard.

PRINTED IN THE UNITED STATES OF AMERICA

9 8 7 6 5 4 3 2 1

Library of Congress Cataloging-in-Publication Data

Geyer, Alan F.
  Lines in the sand : justice and the Gulf War / Alan Geyer and Barbara G. Green ; with a foreword by Kermit D. Johnson. — 1st ed.
        p.   cm.
  Includes bibliographical references and index.
  ISBN 0-664-25301-6

  1. Persian Gulf War, 1991—Moral and ethical aspects. 2. Just war doctrine. I. Green, Barbara G. (Barbara Graham). 1950–
II. Title.
DS79.72.G42   1992
956.704′3—dc20   91-35166

To friends and companions of many years
in the struggle for justice and peace:

Ambassador Olle Dahlén
Politician, Diplomat, Ecumenist

Bishop James K. Mathews
Eunice Jones Mathews
Ministers to the World Parish

Mary Jane Patterson
George Chauncey
Saints of Capitol Hill

Contents

Foreword

Before the Persian Gulf War began, there was a fairly substantive debate among clergy and in the Congress centering on how just war principles ought to be applied to the upcoming war. But once the war started, the debate became muted, since few wished to violate the wartime precepts "support our president" and "support our troops." Perhaps Arnold J. Toynbee was right when he said that war is "an act of religious worship." When people enter the cathedral of violence, they are hushed into silence. Even at war's end, in the din of hallowed victory when high praises are being sung, it seems only a little less sacrilegious to raise questions about the war. But this is what Alan Geyer and Barbara Green have been about, before, during, and after the war.

Not only do they question the basis, conduct, and consequences of the Persian Gulf War, they also question the adequacy of just war theory itself. They challenge us to reopen the moral debate, not only about this particular war but about the whole range of moral principles to which we ought to adhere when considering war and alternatives to it. Thus the scope of their concern: "The principal criteria of the [just war] tradition do not really add up to a complete ethic of war and peace—only an ethic of war. The positive imperatives and strategies of peacemaking—theological, ethical, political—call for something above and beyond just war tradition: the foundations of a just peace." The outlines of this foundational ethic of war and peace appear in the final chapter, and utilize the themes of economic equity, common security, and environmental preservation. Their book is timely and important precisely because just war principles have been so easily used as a justification for war rather than as a presumption against it.

The authors use the Persian Gulf War as a case study through which they reveal misuses and inherent limitations of just war theory. They demonstrate the invalidity of using just war criteria in snapshot fashion for a "go" or "no-go" decision on getting into war. Instead, they place just war considerations in the larger context of "the burdens of history." There is a powerful cumulative effect in their simply laying out the facts concerning events and policies prior to, during, and after the war. At the very least, this longitudinal approach relativizes such moral judgments about involvement in the war as were made by President Bush: "noble," "right," "good," and "moral." No one can read this book without realizing that both sides were caught up in a war filled with deep ambiguities and inextricable evils.

The just war "snapshot" focused on Saddam Hussein's egregious aggression. What did not come into focus were complicities in the background, which the authors point out: "the US-Iran-Iraq triangle, the unrestrained consumption of oil, the disparagement of the United Nations' security role, and the one-sided relationship with Israel." Likewise, the nature of the war and its aftermath call into question the moral claim of proportionality, that the good outweighed

the evil: "the enormity of Iraqi casualties and unending suffering, the environmental disasters, the lost
peace dividend, the disdain for issues of domestic justice, the escalation of the arms trade, the seductive
exhibitionism of high-tech weaponry, the deeper despair of the Palestinians, the aggravation of misery
among the world's poorest peoples . . . ."

Obviously, the authors see all wars, including the
Persian Gulf War, from the perspective and imperatives of a universalistic gospel. This frees them from
using just war principles as an ideological tool to justify national interests. Their interest in all parties involved in the conflict points to the need to utilize the
concept of an ideal ethical observer if just war principles are to be applied fairly. Least of all would such an
attempt at objectivity result in soft-pedaling the
atrocities of Saddam Hussein, nor would it be an ex-
cursion into pacifism. But it would mean a deep rec-
ognition of the humanity of the Iraqi people,
including its soldiers. It would be to say with President Bush: "We have no argument with the people of
Iraq. Indeed, we have only friendship for the people
there." The difference would be that more appropriate ways would be sought to express this friendship
than by killing them. That is what this unsentimental
book is all about—raising the threshold of war to provide space for workable alternatives.

KERMIT D. JOHNSON

August 28, 1991
Reston, Virginia

Preface

On the very day Operation Desert Storm ended, the editors of Westminster/John Knox Press invited us to write "a small book" on the ethical issues of the Gulf War—and to do so "in short order."

This book has been written in short order, but is not quite as small as originally envisioned. As short as the war itself was, the ethical issues surrounding it are many and many-faceted. While the definitive histories of the war will not be written for some years and may reorder our moral perspectives on it, there are immediate and urgent reasons for keeping the churches and the general public focused on both the causes and the consequences of the war. If the war offered, as George Bush repeatedly declared, the "defining moment for a new world order," that moment must not pass without the most thoughtful and most prayerful efforts at definition.

Our subtitle, "Justice and the Gulf War," is intended to suggest such an ethical focus, especially by highlighting both the uses and the limits of the just war tradition in Western and Christian thought. The term "Gulf War" is admittedly problematical in view of the earlier 1980–88 war between Iraq and Iran, in which the United States was peripherally involved. Moreover, the term "Persian Gulf War" is regarded unhappily by Arabs along the same gulf, who prefer the term "Arabian Gulf." In some passages, however, we have capitulated to the most common usages in American cartography, media, and political practice. Whether yet another gulf war is in the making as a consequence of matters left unsettled by "Desert Storm" is a question of profoundest concern just now.

The authors cannot claim legitimate, full-time Middle East expertise. One of us has been intensively engaged in the policy issues of the Gulf War as they have been addressed by the advocacy networks of the churches in Washington. The other has been intermittently preoccupied with the Middle East since a first visit to the region nearly three decades ago, having served as secretary of an ecumenical task force on the Middle East and having taught a bit, written much, and lectured widely on the region's problems (clearly to no avail). The maps have been provided *pro bono publico* by the Geyer Geography Company (GGC), which celebrated its fiftieth anniversary in 1991.

We are grateful to the following persons for reviewing our work and making suggestions for its improvement: Kevin Barr, Mark S. Burrows, Dwain Epps, David Hopkins, Denise Dombkowski Hopkins, Robert Smylie, and J. Philip Wogaman. Kermit Johnson (Major General, retired), former Chief of U.S. Army Chaplains, ordained Presbyterian minister, and longtime colleague in thinking through the most difficult issues of war and peace, kindly agreed to offer the foreword.

To the editors at Westminster/John Knox Press, and especially to Editorial Director Davis Perkins, we are pleased to express deep appreciation for their trust, their confidence, and their most helpful collaboration in the production of this book. The faults which have survived the faithful labors of our editors and reviewers can only be charged to the authors.

ALAN GEYER
BARBARA G. GREEN

1

Ethics
and Desert Storm

In 1922, a British colonial officer named Sir Percy Cox drew some lines in the desert sand to mark the boundaries separating the protectorate of Kuwait from the newly established kingdoms of Iraq and Saudi Arabia.

In 1990, an American president named George Bush drew "a line in the sand" to protect Saudi Arabia from a perceived threat of Iraqi invasion and to initiate measures to force Iraqi withdrawal from Kuwait.

This book is about those lines in the Arab sands drawn nearly seven decades apart by British and American leaders. But it is more than a discussion of cartography. It is a case study in foreign and military policy: a case made extraordinary by its being the first serious international crisis of the post-Cold War era and by the fact that the Persian Gulf War witnessed the largest invasion force since D-Day, 1944, and the heaviest air assault in history.

It is also primarily a case study in Christian ethics. More than any other war of the twentieth century, the Persian Gulf War, in anticipation and in execution, called forth a profusion of sophisticated moral argument and religious discourse. The protracted interval between Iraq's invasion of Kuwait on August 2, 1990, and U.S. initiation of offensive military action on January 16, 1991, offered an unprecedented opportunity for ethical deliberation over policy options. That interval was particularly marked by the invocation of the Western/Christian just war tradition by church bodies, moral theologians, and religious journalists— a tradition that can be (and was) used either to justify the resort to war or to reject it. George Bush made explicit and persistent use of the concepts of the just war tradition in justifying his policies in the Gulf. However, the designation "Operation Just Cause" had already been appropriated for his 1989 invasion of Panama. Thus, the Gulf War, in anticipation, became "Operation Desert Shield"; in execution, "Operation Desert Storm."

Time and Space for Debate

Earlier American wars in this century had not seemed to offer the same time and space for religious and moral debate. World War I became "the war to make the world safe for democracy" only after German attacks on American shipping seemed to compel a declaration of war. World War II, at least for the United States, arrived suddenly, with the Japanese attack on Pearl Harbor. The Korean War was an altogether unexpected conflict perceived as a Sino-Soviet inflammation of the Cold War. The Vietnam War escalated slowly for years before it roused the religious community to serious debate and dissent; even then, the complexities and moral ambiguities of insurgency and counter-insurgency mixed with multiple external interventions vexed most pretensions to rational morality.

The Persian Gulf War was different from all of the

above. Iraq's undeniable aggression met immediate and near-universal condemnation. Nearly half a year would pass, however, before Iraq's military forces were directly attacked. The U.S. government very deliberately planned and mobilized an enormous combination of air, naval, and ground forces; mustered a multinational coalition; and secured United Nations warrants for sanctions, a blockade, and "all necessary means" of military action. Those five and one-half months allowed bishops, church councils, and scholars to reflect at some length on policy alternatives and to invoke theological and ethical perspectives on the Gulf crisis.

It was the extraordinary prominence of Christian just war principles in Gulf War debates that gives shape to much of this book. There are, however, other ethical frameworks for reflecting on the issues of war and peace, and those other frameworks were also employed in the Gulf debates. Moreover, the authors of this volume are persuaded that the just war tradition at best offers only a partial and typically truncated agenda for Christian reflection in matters of war and peace. A more positive and more comprehensive framework has been emerging in the churches in recent years: a theology and ethic for a just peace.

If the five and one-half months between the Iraqi invasion and the U.S. offensive response permitted significant moral debate to take place, the brevity of the six weeks of actual warfare and the unexpectedly swift conclusion of the ground war tended to foreclose debate in the euphoria of the U.S. and Coalition victory. All too quickly, many if not most Americans will let the war and its controversies slip into that abyss of forgetfulness into which we lose our historical consciousness.

We believe the moral debate must go on, with fundamental respect for the patriotism of both the defenders of and dissenters from U.S. policy in the Gulf.

The congressional and public debates before January 16, 1991, demonstrated a capacity for civility-in-controversy in the best tradition of American democracy. A military victory is not necessarily moral vindication, lest we capitulate to the notion that might makes right. A continuing moral debate about the Gulf War may keep us open to reconsideration of alternative courses of action that might have avoided the war, to revelation of truths undisclosed during the war, to reconnaissance of the most serious consequences of the war, and to reflection on the most constructive approaches to justice and peace in the postwar Middle East.

And more: No region in the world is more more-than-regional than the Middle East in its implications for the world as a whole. President Bush portrayed the Gulf crisis as "the defining moment" for a "new world order." While that rhetoric does not necessarily justify administration policies, it hardly exaggerates the global significance of the war. The conspicuous role of the United Nations, the engagement of the superpowers, and the world's dependence on Middle Eastern oil all testify to the ongoing imperative for critical reflection and debate on this conflict.

Alternative Frameworks

Before focusing on the substance of the just war tradition, let us briefly mention four alternative frameworks. Christian pacifists, of course, opposed this war as a matter of faithful principle. But they have also joined the public debate on particular policy issues, even invoking the criteria of the just war tradition to reinforce their opposition, while suggesting that the tradition nevertheless is limited in its depth and breadth and in its demonstrable capacity for restraint. Mennonite pacifist John Howard Yoder acknowledges that the tradition "does serve, some of the time, as an agenda, a checklist of questions which it is fitting to ask in considering war."[1] But Yoder also suggests that the Persian Gulf War tests the tradition itself and finds it lacking in clarity and credibility.

Another framework with ancient sources is that of the *crusade*: the conviction that enemies in a war are more than political adversaries—they are the "enemies of God." Saddam Hussein, who for years styled Iraq as a secular state in contrast to the Islamic theocracy of Iran, affected a "holy war" posture against the United States in calling for Arab solidarity in a *jihad*. While rebuking Saddam Hussein on this point and proclaiming temperate just war principles, President Bush frequently struck a religious posture himself during the war in public addresses, meetings with Christian evangelists, prayer breakfasts, and proclamations of special days of prayer. He thus seemed to impart a religious sanction to the war.

Some persons and groups approach war primarily from the perspective of a radical ideology. War is viewed as the product of capitalist society, or the military-industrial complex, or imperialistic interests. Some of the largest antiwar demonstrations in 1990 and 1991 in Washington and San Francisco were staged by groups on the radical left, for whom specifically religious principles were secondary at best. While the Cold War had ended diplomatically by 1990, its military systems remained fully intact and were available for making war against a new enemy.

Finally, the Gulf War was debated on the grounds of national interest and *realpolitik*, largely devoid of moral or religious rhetoric, if not cynical about moral discourse altogether. Some advocated offensive military action primarily to secure oil interests or to prevent their control by Iraq. Others opposed the war on the understanding that the United States had no vital interests at stake in intervening in an intra-Arab conflict or defending an autocratic emirate. Still others, believing that vital interests were indeed at stake, maintained those interests would be better served by nonmilitary means.

Just War Criteria

A brief restatement of just war principles will suggest most of the policy questions to be discussed in the chapters that follow.

Decisions as to whether it is just to resort to war (*jus ad bellum*) in particular cases are to be guided by the following criteria:

1. There must be a *just cause*, such as resistance to aggression.
2. The aims of the war must be controlled by *just intent*, meaning the restoration of peace with justice rather than self-aggrandizement or vengeful devastation.
3. A decision for war must be a *last resort*, made only after every reasonable means of a just and peaceful settlement has been pursued. (The just war tradition shares with pacifism a moral presumption against going to war.)
4. A decision for war may only be made by *legitimate authority*, whether of a sovereign government or legally competent international organization.
5. A war should not be waged or continued without a *reasonable prospect of success*. It is no act of justice to subject citizens to the suffering and sacrifice of war if that war appears likely to end in failure to achieve the war's right intentions, or in crushing defeat.

If the above criteria are met and a war is commenced, decisions concerning the just conduct of war (*jus in bello*) must meet two additional criteria:

6. The war must honor the principle of *discrimination,* requiring *noncombatant or civilian immunity* from direct attack and the avoidance of massacres, atrocities, looting, and wanton violence.
7. The war's violence must be restrained by the norm of *proportionality*: The war's harm must not exceed the war's good. Justice is violated when suffering, loss of life, and the scale of destruction exceed the minimum of violence required to achieve the war's just intent. (The norm of proportionality also applies to any decision as to whether to wage war at all.)

Limitations of the Tradition

If the just war tradition does offer a useful checklist of significant moral questions, it is necessary to state at the outset of this study our own convictions concerning the tradition's limitations, if only in briefest outline.

The invocation of the just war tradition tends:

1. To obscure the ambiguities of justice in most conflicts, responsibility for which is typically shared by both or all sides.
2. To avoid the imperatives of repentance, usually the precondition of reconciliation and a constraint upon national self-righteousness.
3. To be reactive to the latest provocation, rather than to a whole longitudinal series of historic events (like the football referee who sees and penalizes only the player who reacts to a punch the official has not seen).
4. To presuppose a disjunction between justice and love at the core of Christian ethics, thus elevating love to a level of docetic (disembodied) irrelevance.

5. To define justice in terms of resisting overt military violence and to neglect conditions of systemic and institutional oppression.
6. To justify excessive human suffering and death, euphemistically called "collateral damage," in the conduct of war by appealing to the casuistic principle of "double effect"—that is, by preoccupation with the *intention* of targeting policies to the discounting of their actual *consequences*.
7. To serve as the military ethic of the most powerful nations, rationalizing their policies against weaker powers and tending toward the unacknowledged conceit that might makes right.
8. To reinforce unilateral decision-making in a world of multinational realities and the necessity for common security.

We believe that all these tendencies were exhibited, to some extent, in the United States' conduct of the Persian Gulf War. That judgment, to be developed in the chapters of this book, does not claim to settle all the moral issues of the war. Perhaps similar judgments could be made about the behavior of most governments in most wars. If so, that only strengthens the too-often forgotten presumption the just war tradition shares with pacifism: a presumption against any resort to war. In today's multi-periled world, that presumption needs all the reinforcement it can get.

A final, and most serious, limitation of the just war tradition is its essentially negative preoccupation with questions as to whether, or when, or how to resort to war. The principal criteria of the tradition do not really add up to a complete ethic of war and peace—only to an ethic of war. The positive imperatives and strategies of peacemaking—theological, ethical, political—call for something above and beyond the just war tradition: the foundations of a just peace.

Christian Memory and Repentance

Beyond the limitations of the just war tradition are yet greater burdens of Christian history, especially in the Middle East of Christian origins.

In July 1099, Christian forces captured Jerusalem and slaughtered the Muslim population of the Holy City. The Crusades' assaults on, and plunder of, Muslims in the eleventh to thirteenth centuries are hardly part of American Christian memory these days, but they remain a bitter and never-forgotten story in Muslim memory. The Crusades and the later centuries of imperialism from Western, predominantly Christian nations help to explain why Christian missions have never flourished in Arab lands.

Another people with a heavy sense of history remembers that the Christians of England, France, and Rhineland Germany massacred or expelled their Jewish populations during those very same years of Crusades against the Muslims, thereby preparing for the following centuries of Christian anti-Semitism and the Holocaust.

Christians share a brutal heritage in our relations with both the Muslims and Jews of the Middle East. That sober fact may help us to appreciate the absurdity of an awful moment in the early history of the United Nations. One day, the Israeli ambassador and the Egyptian ambassador, a Jew and a Muslim, engaged in a hot debate and almost came to blows. Whereupon there arose the U.S. ambassador, a pompous former senator, who pleaded: "Gentlemen! Gentlemen! Please settle your differences in a spirit of Christian charity!" It was only after the most painstaking efforts of his staff to explain to him what he had said that the U.S. ambassador requested that his remarks be stricken from the record.

The most appropriate perspective for American

Christians in addressing the ethical issues of the Gulf
War remains confessional. Not only the burdens of
the distant past now compel a confessional stance.
What must not be lost to memory are the many specific entanglements of U.S. policy in the events leading up to Saddam Hussein's August 2, 1990, assault
on Kuwait. We have tried to tell that story in chapter
3, titled "Just Cause? Questions of Complicity." Most
of the other chapters offer additional material for national repentance.

This book remains an invitation to renew the moral
debate about the Gulf War. We have sought to give
voice to both the promoters and critics of U.S. policy
as well as to trace the unfolding of events that have
often confounded almost everyone. We have made no
special effort to conceal our own judgments when we
felt such judgments were warranted—but we have
had to acknowledge all too frequently the need to
know more than we now do about operations Desert
Shield and Desert Storm.

2

Just Cause?
The Roots
of Conflict

In an address to the nation on August 8, 1990, President Bush declared that

> in the early morning hours of August 2, Iraqi armed forces, without provocation or warning, invaded a peaceful Kuwait. Facing negligible resistance from its much smaller neighbor, Iraq's tanks stormed in blitz-krieg fashion through Kuwait in a few short hours. . . . This aggression came just hours after Saddam Hussein specifically assured numerous countries in the area that there would be no invasion. There is no justification whatsoever for this outrageous and brutal act of aggression.

On January 28, 1991, a dozen days after launching the air war against Iraq, President Bush made the claim of just cause explicit in an address to the National Religious Broadcasters Convention:

> The first principle of a just war is that it supports a just cause. Our cause could not be more noble. We seek Iraq's withdrawal from Kuwait, completely, immediately and without condition. . . . We seek nothing for ourselves.

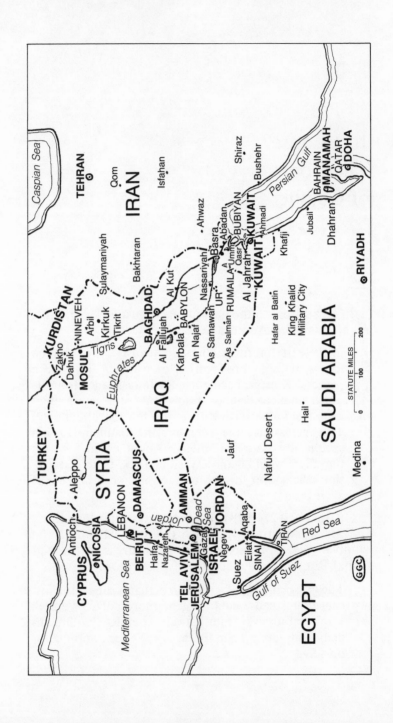

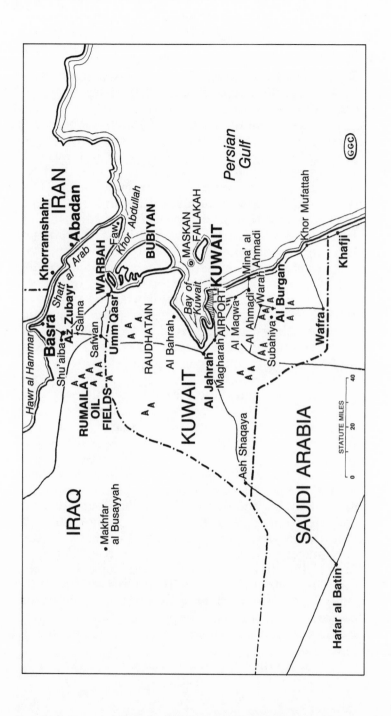

That declaration came after Bush cited saints Ambrose, Augustine, and Thomas Aquinas as expounders of the just war tradition.

This disavowal of any U.S. self-interest would frequently be contradicted in the weeks to come by the president's own appeals to U.S. "vital interests" at stake in the war. However, the sheer perfidy and horror of Iraq's attack on Kuwait are indisputable. Despite Iraq's heavy diplomatic pressure and vague threats against Kuwait between February and July of 1990, Saddam Hussein repeatedly assured Arab and U.S. leaders, right up to the eve of the invasion, that there would be no such attack. The invasion was more than a military occupation of territory: the very identity of Kuwait was to be annihilated. The ruling Al-Sabah family's Dasman Palace, the parliament, and other buildings were destroyed and defiled. Government documents were burned. The Emirate of Kuwait was ceremoniously demoted to "Province 19" of Iraq.

More grisly than these symbolic assaults were the tortures, rapes, and random massacres by Iraqi soldiers and special agents. While some of the atrocity stories were concocted or inflated by Kuwaiti propaganda and rumor mills, there was unquestionably a vast amount of brutal and gratuitous violence. Hotels, homes, libraries, and museums were looted. Half the native Kuwaiti population of eight hundred thousand fled the country, as did hundreds of thousands of Palestinians and other immigrant workers. In the later stages of the war, innumerable Kuwaitis were carted off to Iraq as hostages. Before departure, Iraqi forces set 600 of Kuwait's 950 oil wells on fire, darkening the noonday skies with a smoky preview of nuclear winter and harming air and earth with immeasurable poison, whose effects may last for many years.

Insofar as the U.S. and Coalition case for a just

cause depends on the treacherous and vicious conduct of Iraqi leaders and armed forces, that case is
clear and strong.

But a fully rounded discussion of just cause must
take account of the moral burdens of history: the longitudinal series of events preceding the war, as well as
the historic responsibilities of various nations whose
conduct may have contributed to the conflict. Especially critical to the present moral debate is the question of whether this war and its immense suffering
could have been avoided by more irenic and more
prudent policies by those who claimed just cause
against aggression.

There are both decades-long and short-term issues
of responsibility to be recalled in surveying the full
context of the Persian Gulf War. In most U.S. wars,
the question of war guilt has tended to be foreshort-
ened historically and disclaimed morally by Americans. Typically, the adversaries of the United States
have appealed to a much longer span of historic responsibility.

The Deeper Roots of the Gulf Crisis

The claims and counterclaims of justice in the Gulf
War are implicated in the tangled history of British
imperialism with the Ottoman Empire, as well as in
ancient Christian-Muslim hostilities. For more than
four hundred years, from the fall of Christian Con-
stantinople in 1453 until the early 1900s, the Ottoman Turks held sway over a vast, sprawling Middle
Eastern agglomeration of principalities, sheikhdoms,
and emirates. In the late eighteenth and the nineteenth century, Britain increasingly weakened Ottoman power in order to protect land and sea routes to
India and monopolize Middle Eastern trade.

A key element in British imperial strategy was to
induce local sheikhs and emirs to sign exclusive agree-

ments of trade and protection, thus challenging and
dissipating Ottoman sovereignty. (In recent decades,
that strategy has been resented in the Arab world and
is viewed as a policy designed to destroy Arab unity.)
While the Ottomans considered the mud-brick port of
Kuwait to belong to their Province of Basra, the Al-
Sabah dynasty has actually ruled Kuwait from the
eighteenth century onward. Under pressure from re-
surgent Ottoman power in the late nineteenth century, Sheikh Mubarak Al-Sabah sought British
protection. Kuwait in 1899 thus became a British protectorate in exchange for annual Al-Sabah payments
of fifteen thousand pounds. Ottoman authorities,
however, declined to recognize Kuwait's status as a
protectorate.

The defeat of the Ottoman Turks in World War I
left Britain and France as the dominant powers in the
Middle East. Britain had offered promises of independence to Arab nationalists in return for their wartime
alliance against the Turks. But during the war Britain
had also pledged its support for a Jewish homeland in
Palestine in the famous Balfour Declaration of November 2, 1917, made just five weeks before Turkish
forces surrendered the city of Jerusalem to British
General Edmund Allenby. Thus ended exactly 400
years of Turkish occupation of the Holy City, from
1517 to 1917. And thus the British were implicated in
what Brian Lapping in *End of Empire* has called
"careless promises": permitting "two rival suitors to
believe they had been promised the bride."

In the aftermath of World War I, the British were in
imperial control of most Arab lands: League of Nations "mandates" in Palestine and Trans-Jordan,
Egypt, the ill-defined realms of Iraq and Kuwait, and
numerous sheikhdoms along the Persian Gulf. The
French acquired a League mandate over Syria which
included Lebanon.

It was primarily British policies and decisions in

managing imperial interests that both spurred and frustrated Arab nationalism. For a half-century after 1920, British control yielded piecemeal to at least nominal independence for one Arab country after another: Egypt (1923), Iraq (1932), Jordan (1946), Kuwait (1961), and Bahrain, Qatar, and the United Arab Emirates (1971). But both before and after these sovereignties were proclaimed, Britain sought to maintain and manipulate Arab elites who would support British oil and military concessions. Oil production began in Iraq in the 1920s; in Bahrain, 1932; in Saudi Arabia, 1936; in Qatar, 1940; and in Kuwait, 1946.

The re-emergence of Pan-Arabism in recent decades testifies to historic resentments against imperial policies designed to keep Arab peoples divided and thereby too weak to challenge Western interests.

Beyond outrage at this persistence of colonial and neocolonial interests, Arab nationalism was particularly inflamed by two aspects of British policy: the commitment to Zionism and the arbitrariness of British-imposed boundaries on the Middle East map. These two matters, Zionism and Iraqi borders, became critically linked in Saddam Hussein's rationalizations and Arab sentiments in 1990 and 1991.

Notwithstanding the Balfour Declaration's promise to Arabs that nothing should be done to "prejudice the civil and religious rights of the existing non-Jewish communities" who made up 90 percent of the population of Palestine, Foreign Secretary Arthur Balfour (later Lord Balfour) personally indicated that Arab sentiments were secondary at best:

> The four great powers are committed to Zionism; and Zionism, be it right or wrong, good or bad, is rooted in age-long tradition, in present needs or future hopes, of far profounder import than the desires and prejudices of the 700,000 Arabs who now inhabit that ancient land.[1]

The support of the Balfour Declaration by President Woodrow Wilson (and by President Harry Truman thirty years later), wartime alliances with imperial Britain, and growing American oil interests in the Middle East would all contribute to anti-American attitudes among Arab peoples. In the decades after Israeli independence in 1948, both Zionist and Arab sentiments would be antagonized by American policies that zigzagged between oil interests and a special security alliance with Israel.

The Creation of Iraq

The British policy of fracturing Arab domains and imposing artificial boundaries upon them in the years after World War I was to become directly implicated in the Persian Gulf crisis of 1990–91. The three Ottoman vilayets (districts) of Baghdad, Basra, and Mosul were separated from Turkey, Syria, Trans-Jordan, and Kuwait and were combined into a new Kingdom of Iraq in 1922—but under a British League of Nations mandate that lasted until 1932. Many years later, Sir Anthony Parsons (former U.N. ambassador and long-time diplomat in the Middle East) bluntly acknowledged that "We, the British, cobbled Iraq together. It was always an artificial state; it had nothing to do with the people who lived there."[2]

Of course, Iraqi memory could stretch back beyond the British, Ottoman, and even Mongol conquests to reclaim the imperial power and glory of the Caliphate of Baghdad, with its vast domains in the eighth and ninth centuries. Even more, Iraqi cultural pride could always evoke the splendors of Mesopotamian civilizations of 2,500 to 5,000 years ago: Ur, Nineveh, Nippur, and Babylon.

It took more than three decades for modern Iraq to free itself completely from the British colonial yoke. King Feisal, a British protégé of the Hashemite family, which would also rule Jordan, acquiesced in the maintenance of British military bases and an oil monopoly that would persist until 1958. In that year, a radical anti-Western, pan-Arab revolution under General Abdul Karem Kassem overthrew the monarchy and proclaimed a new Republic of Iraq. The British were forced to abandon their military bases in Iraq.

It was in November of 1922, the year of Iraq's formation as a British mandate, that the British High Commissioner, Sir Percy Cox, drew the lines in the sand marking the borders of Iraq, Kuwait, and Saudi Arabia. At a tent meeting in the Arabian desert, the Saudi sheikh who would soon become King Ibn Saud humbly accepted the British decrees from Sir Percy, as did the British political agent representing Kuwait and a junior official from Iraq. The prescribed borders not only definitively severed Kuwait from southern Iraq but also denied Iraq any secure access to the Persian Gulf. The British clearly wanted to keep Iraq as nearly landlocked as possible so as to deny Iraq any effective challenge to British control of the Gulf. Sir Anthony Parsons recalled: "We protected our strategic interests rather successfully, but in doing so we didn't worry too much about the people living there. We created a situation where people felt they had been wronged."[3] Iraq was left with the west bank of the Shatt al-Arab, the estuary of the Tigris and Euphrates whose east bank was largely under Iranian sovereignty.

Claims to Kuwait

While pre-World War I British maps clearly show their protectorate of Kuwait lying beyond the outer boundaries of the Ottoman empire, the Ottoman Turks drew their maps differently. Kuwait was still claimed by the Turks as a part of their Basra district.

After Iraqi independence in 1932, Iraqi leaders appealed to Ottoman maps and unsuccessfully tried various stratagems to annex or confederate with Kuwait. When Kuwait declared its full independence in 1961 and the British protectorate ended, Iraq not only refused to recognize Kuwait but massed troops on its border in preparation for an invasion. Premier Kassem told a Baghdad news conference that Kuwait was "an integral part of Iraq." The invasion and takeover were prevented by a swift return of British forces, which was regarded by Iraq as "an aggression of Iraq's territory and an overt foreign intervention in the affairs of the Arab world." The Soviet Union agreed, charging the British with another attempt to split the Arab world.[4]

It was not until 1963 that Iraq finally recognized the independence of Kuwait—but it did so without recognizing the specific lines in the sand drawn by Sir Percy Cox in 1922. The two unending border disputes concern access to the Gulf and control of oil fields. Kuwait, with its own secure ports on the Gulf, has also claimed sovereignty over the strategic islands of Warbah and Bubiyan which block access to the Khor Abdullah, the waterway that leads to the Iraqi port of Umm Qasr. The Rumaila oil fields along the northwest border of Kuwait have been pumped by both countries without any clear comity agreement.

While many Iraqis, including exiles who have fled Saddam Hussein's brutal regime, opposed the cruel invasion of Kuwait, they are nonetheless inclined to share Iraq's claims to at least portions of Kuwait. Those claims are based upon historic grievances against British imperialism and the arbitrariness of the lines in the sand. Shortly after Saddam Hussein's invasion, an Iraqi political scientist in exile in London declared: "It's not Saddam's problem or Saddam's cause; it's every Iraqi's cause, even those, who like myself, are against Saddam and believe the invasion was totally wrong."[5]

So: For decades Iraqis generally have believed they had a just cause against Western imperialism and its outposts in both Kuwait and Israel. No doubt they have believed just as passionately in their cause as Americans who believed their war against Iraq was a just cause.

Why Did Iraq Invade Kuwait?

If Saddam Hussein could invoke these old grievances of Iraqi and other Arab peoples in justification of his assault upon Kuwait, he surely had more immediate impulses toward an invasion. In 1989 and 1990, those impulses stemmed from a virtually bankrupt economy in the wake of the eight-year war with Iran; the unimpaired wealth of next-door-neighbor Kuwait, a tiny defenseless city-state that was proving increasingly unresponsive and even scornful toward Iraq's plight; the persisting extremes of wealth and poverty throughout the Arab world, with the wealth concentrated in conservative monarchies; a compound of paranoia and demagoguery concerning the threat of another Israeli attack and an alleged "imperialist-Zionist conspiracy" against Iraq; temptations to rally pan-Arab sentiment in a renewed campaign for Palestinian statehood.

Saddam Hussein sought to portray himself as a new Nasser: the most powerful leader of Pan-Arabism against a host of enemies, including Islamic fundamentalism, Zionism, imperialism, and imperialism's legacies in the oil-rich sheikhdoms of the Persian Gulf. But he confronted such humbling economic circumstances by 1990 that his very political survival was at stake.

Iraq's war against Iran may have cost as much as

$500 billion. Postwar economic troubles could be measured in an $80 billion foreign debt, heavy repayment delinquencies, steep inflation, and $200 billion or more in reconstruction costs.

Saddam Hussein assailed Arab League members with a variety of desperate appeals, demands, and threats in the first half of 1990. He sought forgiveness of Iraq's debts, new grants and credits, higher oil prices, adherence to OPEC quotas, and compensation from Kuwait for exploitation of disputed oil fields.

During and after the war with Iran, Saddam Hussein had tried to persuade Kuwait and the other Gulf states to forgive Iraqi debts, claiming that Iraq had borne the burden of a common Arab cause (a cause supported by the United States) to prevent the militant expansion of Islamic fundamentalism, Khomeini-style. Having met rejection, he demanded at a February 1990 meeting of the Arab Cooperation Council that Iraq be granted not only a moratorium on wartime loans but also $30 billion in immediate relief. These demands were reinforced by implied threats against Kuwait and Saudi Arabia, followed by a show of military maneuvers along the Kuwaiti border. An unintimidated Kuwait pointedly refused to make concessions.

Saddam Hussein was also caught in a fierce battle over oil prices. Iraq tried to persuade OPEC to reduce oil production quotas in order to force oil prices and income to rise. Kuwait and the United Arab Emirates not only rejected the proposal but increased their own production far above their allotted quotas, thus contributing to an oil glut and falling prices. Perhaps exaggerating, Iraq claimed the glutted oil market had cost its own economy an additional $89 billion.[6]

This intra-Arab oil war came to a climax at the Arab Summit in Baghdad in May of 1990. In a closed session, Saddam Hussein confronted the visiting heads of state with the urgency of Iraq's predicament: "For every single dollar drop in the price of a barrel of oil, our loss amounts to $1 billion a year." He went on to charge that the violation of oil quotas by Gulf states amounted to a virtual declaration of war against Iraq: a war "by economic means."

> Were it possible, we would have endured. But I believe that all our brothers are fully aware of our situation. . . . We have reached a point where we can no longer withstand pressure.

In a bitter exchange with Saddam Hussein, the Emir of Kuwait refused to cut oil production, or forgive war loans, or extend further grants to Iraq, or make territorial concessions.[7]

That May summit may have convinced Saddam Hussein that the seizure of Kuwait was his last resort—particularly if he could assume that such an invasion could be executed with little resistance and would be irreversible. He could appeal to the old Ottoman and modern Iraqi claims that Kuwait really belonged to the Basra province and was only an artificial city-state fabricated by imperial Britain. Much would depend on the attitude of the "imperialists" in 1990, especially the United States, Britain, and France.

At a July 10 meeting of oil ministers in Jeddah, Saudi Arabia, Kuwait finally yielded to joint Saudi-Iranian-Iraqi pressure to adhere to oil production quotas—but still would not forgive or extend loans. On July 16, Iraq's Foreign Minister Tariq Aziz charged that Kuwait was stealing oil from Iraq's own Rumaila oil field on their border, a "theft" that had cost Iraq $2.4 billion in lost income. This charge was backed up by four demands: (1) that Kuwait stop "stealing" Iraqi oil and also compensate Iraq for the lost $2.4 billion; (2) that Iraq be granted a moratorium on repayment of wartime loans; (3) that OPEC oil prices be raised to at least $25 a barrel; and (4) that Iraq be the recipient of an Arab "Marshall Plan" as compensation for wartime losses versus Iran.[8]

The next day, July 17, Saddam Hussein, in a public address, accused Gulf states of stabbing Iraq in the back with "a poison dagger" by exceeding OPEC oil quotas—and that in a conspiracy "inspired by America to undermine Arab interests and security."

On July 18 Kuwait indignantly repudiated all Iraqi claims and demands, apparently doubting the credibility of Iraqi threats. Saddam Hussein thus faced both economic disaster domestically and political humiliation internationally at the hands of a mini-state monarchy with only one-twentieth the area and one-tenth the population of Iraq—but with half the GNP, the same volume of exports, and more than five times the per capita income.

On July 20, Iraq began to deploy 100,000 troops on the Kuwaiti border. If Saddam Hussein's primary motives for seizing Kuwait were to capture Kuwait's wealth and thereby to overcome his economic crisis and survive politically, he could adorn those motives with appeals to Arab masses' resentment of the inordinate wealth of Gulf mini-states and the plight of the Palestinians under Israeli occupation. By 1990, Kuwait, Qatar, and the United Arab Emirates all enjoyed paternalistic welfare states with per capita incomes of $10,000–$30,000. By contrast, Iraq's per capita income is only about $2,000; Egypt's, less than $1,000.

There is no good reason to believe that the grievances of the Palestinians against Israel served as the main motive for Iraq's seizure of Kuwait. However, Saddam Hussein preached linkage between these two issues in order to enlist wider Arab support for his invasion. Saddam Hussein also attempted to provoke Israel into becoming a major belligerent, and thereby to enlist most Arab states into a wartime alliance that might annihilate Israel. While Israelis were dismayed at the spectacle of Palestinian cheers for Iraq's Scud missile attacks on Israel, this gambit caused few casualties and little damage. Israeli leaders understood the gambit and, to the surprise of many (and the frustration of Saddam Hussein), declined to retaliate with more than rhetoric.

Iraq's security concerns, however, were genuinely linked to Israel's policies. After all, in 1981 Israel had attacked and destroyed Iraq's Osirak nuclear reactor near Baghdad, claiming that Iraq was developing nuclear weapons. Israel, on the other hand, had covertly developed its own nuclear arms arsenal—an obvious threat to Iraq and other Arab states who understandably remained furious that Israel would apparently resort to any means to prevent parity in military technology in the region. On a personal visit to Baghdad in February 1990, Richard Murphy (who had been Assistant Secretary of State for Near Eastern Affairs under President Reagan) was informed that Israel was apparently planning a strike against Iraq's nonconventional arms industries. In March, Gerald Bull, a Canadian ballistic missile expert who was helping Iraq develop a long-range "supergun," was assassinated in Brussels—a deed later acknowledged by Mossad, Israel's security service.

So Saddam Hussein had good reason to feel threatened by Israel. Addressing the General Command of his armed forces on April 2, the Iraqi president denied that he would develop nuclear weapons, candidly preferring the possible use of chemical weapons against Israel in response to an Israeli attack. Western governments, he asserted, "will be deluded if they imagine that they can give Israel a cover in order to come and strike at some industrial metalworks. By God, we will make fire eat half of Israel if it tries to do anything against Iraq." But he added that he had no intention of attacking Israel first—a pledge he later said he would renounce in the event of a Western attack upon Iraq after the occupation of Kuwait.[9]

It is possible to suppose, therefore, that Saddam

Hussein's immediate motives for seizing Kuwait were primarily a matter of economic desperation and political survival, but that he also imagined a wider conflict in which he would emerge as the new Super Sheikh of pan-Arab nationalism, the champion of the Palestinians, and the final victor over Israel and Western imperialism.

Whatever the true weight of these issues of historic grievance, economic justice, and human rights, the fact remains that Kuwait was and is a sovereign member of the United Nations. Iraq recognized Kuwaiti sovereignty in 1963. Iraq's invasion was clearly an act of aggression. The plunder of Kuwait and the cruelties inflicted upon the people of Kuwait can hardly merit the name of justice.

3

Just Cause?
Questions
of Complicity

It is not an easy matter for Americans to acknowledge historic complicity in the causes of any war. We
are too fond of believing in the benevolence of American purposes and the innocence of American interests. Our "moral exceptionalism" and our messianic
pretensions as a "nation under God" make candid
self-appraisal difficult at best. Moreover, our political
culture of historical indifference ill equips us to recall
our own past patterns of interaction with other peoples whose traumatic memories, memories that are
intergenerational and even ancient, are fundamental
to their sense of nationhood.

A willingness even to contemplate the possibility of
American complicity in the causes of the Persian Gulf
War may be encouraged by examining the question of
culpability in several past wars.

The Mexican War of 1846–48 gave vent to shrill
jingoism and zeal for the nation's "Manifest Des-
tiny." That war resulted in Mexico's loss of California, Nevada, Utah, Colorado, Arizona, New Mexico,
Wyoming, and all claims to Texas north of the Rio
Grande: it was the largest U.S. acquisition of territory

except the Louisiana purchase. It was preceded by a remarkably indulgent inaugural address in 1845 by President James Polk:

> Foreign powers do not seem to appreciate the true character of our government. Our Union is a confederation of independent states whose policy is peace with each other and all the world. Therefore, to enlarge its limits, is to extend the dominions of peace over additional territories and increasing millions. The world has nothing to fear from military ambition in our government.

Senator Henry Clay, however, described the Mexican War as an "unnecessary and offensive aggression" by the United States. "It is Mexico that is defending her firesides, her castles, and her altars, not we." Congressman Abraham Lincoln charged that "the war with Mexico was unnecessarily and unconstitutionally commenced by the President." Lincoln accused Polk of the "sheerest deception," adding that "the blood of this war, like the blood of Abel, is crying to heaven against him." Mexicans have never forgotten or forgiven the United States for that war.

The Spanish-American War of 1898, resulting in U.S. acquisition of the Philippines and Puerto Rico as well as domination of Cuba, was largely a consequence of "yellow journalism" in a circulation war between Hearst and Pulitzer newspapers. There was wholesale fabrication of Spanish "atrocities" and of never-proved Spanish responsibility for sinking the U.S. battleship *Maine* in Havana harbor. There was also an evangelistic and anti-Catholic enthusiasm for the war on the part of Methodist President William McKinley, who declared that Americans had no alternative but "to take them all, and educate the Filipinos, and uplift and civilize them, and by God's grace to do the very best we could for them, as our fellow men for whom Christ also died."

There is a strange split in America's moral consciousness of the causes of World War II: a split between outraged innocence and haunting guilt. On one hand, that war is commonly recalled as the most undebatable example of a just war, given the horrors of Nazism and the treachery of Japan. On the other hand, many older Americans feel unending guilt about U.S. isolationism and keep recalling "the Munich analogy" (a national confession that the war could have been prevented had the United States and the Allies acted together in the 1930s to resist the threats of aggression). Virtually every military move made by the United States since 1945 has been promoted to the public by manipulation of this national guilt over isolationism.

It is important to keep such moral ambiguities in mind when assessing the causes of conflict in the Middle East.

Hard Questions and Second Thoughts

Early in the Persian Gulf crisis of 1990–91, when congressional committees sought to assess past U.S. policies that may have contributed to the crisis, Secretary of State James Baker objected that raising such questions could undermine U.S. efforts to recruit a coalition against Iraq. When the U.S. air offensive was launched on January 16, 1991, congressional and media criticism of prewar policies virtually ceased. When the swift victory came, the euphoria was such that would-be critics of past policies sought to share the triumphal limelight.

Within a few weeks of the cease-fire, however, the hard questions of possible U.S. culpability began to surface. They came less from politicians than from mainstream media. *Time* magazine pointed to a record of "missed signals, interagency disputes, intelligence failures, errors of judgment and flights of

wishful thinking" that contributed to the Gulf crisis.[1]
Newsweek declared: "In all the euphoria over
America's triumph in the Gulf, one thing shouldn't be
forgotten: this war could have been avoided." There
followed an indictment of the United States for its
arms exports, energy policies, "human intelligence,"
neglect of human rights, and obsession with Iran.[2]
The Washington Post published a long critique of
President Bush and Secretary of State Baker for having managed foreign policy in 1989 and 1990 "in an
intensely personal and informal fashion," for largely
ignoring career professionals, for being preoccupied
with the dramas of Soviet and European affairs and,
finally, for being "blindsided by Iraq's invasion of
Kuwait."[3]

Here too, however, are deeper historical roots than
even the second-guessing media uncovered. Those
roots have to do with the first years of the Cold War in
the late 1940s and early 1950s; covert operations in
Iran; U.S. policies toward Israel and the Palestinians;
and the U.S. role in the United Nations.

The Iran Connection

In the long view of U.S. relations with Iraq, nothing
is more crucial than reconstructing the history of a
disastrous triangle: United States-Iran-Iraq. Affecting
that political triangle has been a trio of American ob-
sessions in the Middle East: cheap oil, anticommu-
nism, and dread of Islamic revolution.

The doleful legacy of U.S. policies concerning Iran
from the late 1940s through the 1970s became the
pretext for the policy blunders concerning Iraq in the
1980s. Those blunders in turn formed the immediate
background of the Persian Gulf War. To put it plainly,
the United States helped to create two militarily top-
heavy rival regimes that impoverished and terrorized
their own peoples, menaced their neighbors, and dev-

astated each other in one of the ghastliest wars in this century. Once again, our focus is on the moral burdens of history.

In August of 1953, the Iranian nationalist government of Mohammed Mossadegh was overthrown in a military coup supported by the Shah and engineered by the U.S. Central Intelligence Agency. The coup followed a two-year crisis over oil interests, specifically the British-owned Anglo-Iranian Oil Company, which Mossadegh had nationalized in 1951. Mossadegh's nationalist revolution provided the first serious challenge to Western control of Middle East oil. However, his temporary tactical alliance with communists in the Tudeh Party provided the United States and Britain with the pretext they needed to overthrow him. Britain imposed a financial and commercial blockade on Iran and the United States suspended foreign aid.

While the CIA has never officially acknowledged its part in the Iranian counterrevolution, the "company's" unofficial historians have recounted the prominent roles of two men with very familiar names: Kermit "Kim" Roosevelt and Brigadier General H. Norman Schwarzkopf. Roosevelt, grandson of President Theodore Roosevelt, was the CIA's top operator in the Middle East in the early 1950s and the director of 1953 coup operations. Afterward, he left government service and was rewarded with a position in Washington as "director of government relations" for Gulf Oil, later becoming Gulf's vice-president.

General Schwarzkopf had been well known as the head of the New Jersey State Police in the 1930s who investigated the Lindbergh baby kidnapping case. Many older Americans recall his homilies on the popular "Gang Busters" radio show. He had also reorganized the Shah's police force in the 1940s. His role in the 1953 coup reportedly included the distribution of millions of CIA dollars. General H. Norman Schwarzkopf's name was reincarnated in his son, the "Stormin'

Norman" who headed Operation Desert Storm in 1991—another operation in which Western oil interests were clearly at stake.[4]

After the 1953 coup, five American oil companies (Gulf, Texaco, Socony-Mobil, Standard Oil of New Jersey and Standard Oil of California) joined an international consortium to produce and market Iranian oil. By the mid-1950s, American companies owned 40 percent of Iranian oil, 25 percent of the Iraq Petroleum Company, 50 percent of Kuwaiti oil, and 100 percent of Saudi Arabian oil.[5] For the next quarter century, the United States replaced Britain as protector of the Shah, building up Iran's military forces through the anti-Soviet CENTO (Central Treaty Organization) alliance and $20 billion in armaments.

Repression and corruption under Shah Mohammad Reza Pahlavi were accompanied by mounting anti-American sentiments, leading to massive protests, the exile of the Shah, and the Islamic revolution under Ayatollah Ruhollah Khomeini in 1979. The seizure of the U.S. embassy and sixty-two American hostages on November 4, 1979, led to a break in U.S. diplomatic relations. Iran, with U.S.-supplied military might but now in the grip of Islamic fundamentalism, thus became the major adversary of U.S. policies in the Middle East, having labeled the United States as "the Great Satan."

The Tilt Toward Iraq

U.S.-militarized, fundamentalist Iran also was perceived by Iraq and the Gulf states as the major threat to their own security. The United States thereupon switched sides after the outbreak of the Iraq-Iran War in September 1980. Now it was time to promote the military buildup of Iraq as the "counterbalance to the Iranians," in the words of Zbigniew Brzezinski, National Security Adviser under President Carter. Similarly, Graham Fuller, a CIA official during the Reagan years, recalls:

> There was a genuine visceral fear of Islam in Washington as a force that was utterly alien to American thinking, and that really scared us. Senior people at the Pentagon and elsewhere were much more concerned about Islam than communism. It was almost obsessive fear, leading to a mentality on our part that you should use any stick to beat a dog—to stop the advance of Islamic fundamentalism.[6]

With Iraq as the stick to beat Iran, the United States, France, Germany, Italy, China, and Brazil all added to the Soviet-supplied arsenals of Iraq during the 1980s. The total volume of arms and military equipment that poured into Iraq perhaps equaled the $20 billion the U.S. had earlier exported to Iran. From 1985 to 1990, the U.S. sold Iraq $1.5 billion worth of military equipment and high technology items. Among those items were advanced computers used to develop ballistic missiles, a sale which proceeded over the protests of Stephen Bryen, Deputy Under Secretary of Defense for Trade and Security Policy in the Reagan administration. Recently, Bryen reflected soberly on the consequences of such unguarded policies toward Iraq: "We created this monster. If you want to know who's to blame for all this, we are, because we let all this stuff go to Iraq."[7] The day before the Iraqi invasion of Kuwait, the Bush administration was still at it, approving the sale of $695,000 in advanced data transmission devices to Saddam Hussein's government.[8]

At stake in U.S. exports to Iraq were the profits of such American companies as Hewlett-Packard, Hughes Aircraft, and Bell Aerospace. But there were other economic interests involved in the tilt toward Iraq during the 1980s. Iraq became the biggest single importer of U.S. rice as well as a major importer of corn and wheat. These imports were underwritten by U.S. Export-Import Bank loans and credit guarantees from the Commodity Credit Corporation, reportedly totaling over $4 billion.

The major advocate of a pro-Iraq policy, U.S. commercial interests in Iraq, and U.S. credits and loans to Iraq from 1982 to 1990 was the U.S.–Iraq Business Forum, a coalition of more than fifty firms including Westinghouse, Caterpillar, Amoco, Mobil, General Motors, Xerox, and First City Bancorporation of Texas. Marshall W. Wiley, a lobby lawyer and former ambassador to Oman, has been president of the Forum. Mary E. King, former associate director of ACTION during the Carter administration, has been the executive director. That Forum, working closely with the Iraqi Embassy and engaging the consulting services of Henry Kissinger Associates, persistently opposed sanctions against Iraq in the face of Saddam Hussein's repressions and gas attacks that killed thousands of Kurds in August 1988.[9]

This combination of perceived security interests and the economic interests of arms makers, high tech firms, oil companies, and farm lobbies, all at stake in Iraq, helps to explain why the Reagan-Bush administration never seriously challenged the worst horrors of the Saddam Hussein regime before 1990. Political tyranny, murderous purges, chemical warfare not only against Iran but against Iraq's own Kurdish citizens: these were reason enough for U.S. policy to make forceful representations on human rights issues, to impose sanctions, and to dissociate the U.S. more conspicuously from Saddam Hussein. However, U.S. policy not only emphasized "normal" relations with Iraq but shared secret military intelligence about Iran, promoted grain sales to help feed Iraqi troops and commercial ventures in profitable postwar reconstruction, and apologized for an unauthorized Voice of America broadcast that criticized abuses by Iraqi secret police. Saddam Hussein could hardly have anticipated that George Bush would characterize him as "worse than Adolf Hitler."

A Prodigal Energy Policy

President Bush's motives for going to war against Iraq belong to the next chapter's discussion of *just intent* and therefore of war aims. Here let it be noted that the lack of a disciplined U.S. energy policy during the 1980s, with more than 40 percent of the nation's oil imports continuing to come from the Middle East, surely predisposed U.S. policymakers toward military action in the face of threats to such supplies.

"Linkage" with the Palestinians and Israel

Saddam Hussein's anti-Israel rhetoric, Scud missile attacks on Israel, and embrace of the Palestinian cause failed to make credible "linkage" with his rationale for invading Kuwait. However, U.S. policies toward Israel and the Palestinians in the 1980s provided substantial linkage with the Gulf crisis as it moved toward war in 1990. The intensity of the hostility between Iraq and Israel, as we have noted, is attributable in part to rival nuclear capabilities. The hostility is magnified by the widespread Arab conviction that Israel is a Western imperial intrusion on Arab land, that Israel's own policies are aggressively expansionist, and that the United States is Israel's imperial protector. But Arab antipathy to Israel has been rubbed raw by the continuing denial of a homeland to the Palestinians and the harshness of Israel's repression of Palestinian life and liberties.

It is the inconstancy of U.S. support for Palestinian self-determination, combined with a generally accommodating posture toward Israeli policies, that has

provided Saddam Hussein and other Arab leaders
with much of their political ammunition. The Arab
summit in Baghdad in May 1990, previously noted as
the climax of the oil quota and pricing controversy
between Iraq and Kuwait, was reportedly convened at
the request of Yasir Arafat, head of the PLO (Palestine Liberation Organization). Arafat sought unified
Arab action against the increasing encroachment of
Jewish settlements on the West Bank, which he regarded as inimical to any possibility of establishing an
independent Palestinian state. Summit leaders
adopted a resolution that rebuked the United States
for failing to "further the political process and end
Israeli rule over the territories, despite the valiant
struggle, with its high price in blood, being waged day
in and day out by the Palestinians in the territories"
(the *intifada*). The resolution added that U.S. "military resources, financial aid and political backing"
were the mainstay of Israel's oppressive policies.

For decades now, the obvious requirement of
peacemaking in the Israeli-Palestinian conflict has
been maintaining a sensitive balance between two
principles: Israeli security and Palestinian self-determination. The Camp David Accords of September 17, 1978 (signed by Jimmy Carter, Anwar Sadat,
and Menachem Begin), offered a somewhat ambiguous balance between these two principles, with greater
clarity on security (paving the way for Israel's 1979
peace treaty with Egypt) than on self-determination.
Nevertheless, the Accords did provide for "transitional arrangements" leading to "full autonomy" and
a freely elected "self-governing authority" for the
Palestinians in the West Bank and Gaza. These goals
were to be achieved in "a period not exceeding five
years."

These goals were not achieved by 1983, or by 1991.
William B. Quandt, a National Security Council official present at Camp David, has acknowledged that the

Accords "papered over rather than resolved the vital questions of sovereignty, Jerusalem, and Palestinian self-determination."[10] If Camp David represented a triumph of personal and interfaith diplomacy for Jimmy Carter, even the high point of his presidency, it was a flawed triumph. Quandt adds: "Sadat and Begin both recognized, in a way that Carter initially did not, that Israel would have a free hand in dealing with the Palestinian issue once Egypt had signed a treaty with Israel."[11]

Not many weeks after Camp David, an Arab summit in Baghdad condemned the Accords and condemned Egypt for agreeing to them. Most Arab leaders viewed the Accords as one more Western strategy to divide and weaken the Arab world, and saw Egypt as breaking the ranks of Arab unity. When progress in implementing the pledges of "self-governing" for the Palestinians was not forthcoming, the PLO came to resent Camp David as a disaster for its cause. Ironically, Yitzhak Shamir, who opposed Begin and the Accords in 1978, became their firm advocate as prime minister in the 1980s, precisely because of their permissive ambiguity.

In fairness to Jimmy Carter, his reelection in 1980 (doomed by Ayatollah Khomeini) might well have been followed by a steadfast effort to make good on the vague pledges to the Palestinians. It was not so with Ronald Reagan. Disposed to view the Middle East in a Cold War frame, disinclined to take diplomatic initiatives (even when confronted with a parade of Arab leaders urging him to do so) but occasionally given to fitful and ill-considered gambits, disengaged from his aides, who pursued ill-advised policies, Reagan's stewardship of Middle East affairs was a heavy burden for that region and his own successors to bear.

Reagan's fervently pro-Israel rhetoric, his association with zealously pro-Israel televangelists, his unwillingness to exert leverage on behalf of the Palestinians, and his 1985 disavowal of Palestinian

independence won him strong support from some
U.S. Jewish leaders and Israeli officials, but increasingly alienated Arab governments and Palestinian
leaders. The Israeli line hardened in its control over
the West Bank and Gaza, multiplication of settlements on the West Bank, repression of Palestinians,
and attacks on Palestinians abroad. The Camp David
Accords ceased to be a platform for Palestinian self-
determination; they became instead an infinite source
of obfuscation and evasion.

Israel's invasion of Lebanon on June 6, 1982, which
was plotted by Minister of Defense Ariel Sharon but
employed U.S.-supplied weapons and was implicitly
endorsed by Secretary of State Alexander Haig, had
particularly grievous consequences for Lebanese, for
Palestinians, for Americans, and for Israelis. The invasion was aimed not only at expelling Palestinian
forces operating from Lebanon but also routing Syrian influence and propping up a Maronite Christian
regime under Bashir Gemayel in Beirut. In the chaos
that followed, Israeli forces attacked Syrian forces,
Beirut was heavily bombed by Israel, and Gemayel
was assassinated. Israeli troops in Beirut permitted
the massacre of hundreds of Palestinian refugees in
the Sabra and Shatila camps by Christian Phalangist
troops. Lebanese governmental authority disinte-
grated, and Christian and Muslim militias resumed
their civil war. Terrorist bombings at the U.S. Embassy killed fifty people and 241 U.S. Marines, who
were deployed in an exposed position without clear
policy guidance. Americans and other Westerners
were murdered or made hostage. Israeli forces eventually withdrew from Lebanon under international
pressure. Egypt, having so recently made its peace
with Israel, was politically mortified, and was beset
with Islamic fundamentalist rallies fervent with anti-
Zionism and anti-Americanism and accused of culpability by other Arab states (President Hosni Mubarak

recalled his ambassador from Tel Aviv and refused for four years to resume normal relations with Israel). Syria emerged as the dominant power in Lebanon.

Seldom in modern history has a military venture boomeranged as badly as Israel's 1982 invasion of Lebanon—unless it was Iraq's 1990 invasion of Kuwait. The United States, as Israel's prime sponsor, shared heavily in the opprobrium connected with the chaos in Lebanon. U.S.-Israel relations were badly strained for some months. The Sabra-Shatila massacre became a grisly symbol of injustice to the Palestinians. On a 1984 visit to the Soviet Union, the authors of this book saw propaganda posters in which alleged U.S.-Israeli butchery was graphically (that is, bloodily) depicted as responsible for the massacre.

The many-sided disaster in Lebanon opened wide an impassioned debate within Israel about military policies, the morality of war, and the rights of the Palestinians. Throughout the 1980s, in fact, there were more, and more serious, challenges to Israeli policies within Israel than there were in the United States, where the Reagan administration preferred to avoid responsibility and where most politicians of both parties tended to run shy of offending the pro-Israel lobby. The Labor Party in Israel was more open to negotiations with the PLO, trading land for peace, and holding a comprehensive international conference on Middle East issues. But apart from a brief turn of alternating leadership in a "National Unity" coalition which collapsed in early 1990, the Labor Party lost parliamentary strength to a right-wing coalition under Yitzhak Shamir's Likud Party that rejected negotiations with the PLO and any "land for peace" arrangements, as well as a broad international conference. Moreover, the emergence of the Palestinian *intifada* in 1987 was met by Shamir's government with hundreds of killings and with beatings, burning of Palestinian homes, closing of schools, severe curfews, and other harsh measures.

In sum, over the past decade, as Israeli policies became more intransigent and the cause of the Palestinians became more desperate, the United States
government has failed to sustain a peacemaking strategy for this core conflict of the Middle East. A brief
but token dialogue with the PLO was begun in the last
days of the Reagan administration—but was broken
off by the Bush administration after an abortive Palestinian raid on May 30, 1990, on the Israeli coast, led
by Abul Abbas of the factional Palestine Liberation
Front. (That raid may have come not from the insti-
gation of Yasir Arafat but from that of Saddam Hussein, who wanted an end to U.S.-PLO dialogue and
who was soliciting Palestinian support in the escalating Gulf crisis.)[12] Periodically there were mild U.S.
rebukes of Israeli excesses. But U.S. policy, for the
most part, was determined more in Jerusalem than in
Washington.

By default, the United States gave Saddam Hussein
his most incendiary weapon in the Gulf War: the exploitation of Palestinian grievances. The Palestinians,
having despaired of U.S. and Israeli policies, rallied
to Saddam's side—and thereby became heavy losers:
losers in Palestine, where Israeli authorities virtually
shut down the economy; losers in Jordan, where the
nation was burdened with hundreds of thousands of
refugees from Iraq and had been punished by the suspension of aid from the United States and Saudi Arabia because King Hussein dared to criticize the U.S.
air assault on Iraqi cities; and losers in Kuwait, where
Palestinians had provided an underclass of workers
for well-to-do Kuwaitis. It remains to be seen whether
Palestinian statehood is more a lost cause than ever.

United Nations Peacekeeping

In July 1990, the United Nations, with no established police or peacekeeping force to dispatch to the

area, was faced with the buildup of Iraqi forces on the Kuwaiti border. Had there been such a force, the invasion might have been averted. Or the deployment of such a force on the Saudi Arabian border after the Iraqi occupation of Kuwait might have precluded the massive U.S. intervention. It is the authoritative multinational, symbolic character of such a U.N. force, not its size or its weapons, that could make it capable of decisive interposition in such conflict situations. Most Arab governments, in contrast with Israel, have wanted the U.N. to play a prominent role in Middle East peacemaking and peacekeeping.

More than two decades ago, the Commission to Study the Organization of Peace—a who's who of distinguished U.S. diplomats, scholars, and civic leaders—proposed the establishment on a step-by-step basis of an array of peacekeeping instruments:

1. A Peace Observation Corps to establish a United Nations "presence" in any place where the peace is threatened.
2. A U.N. "fire brigade" of five thousand specially trained and well-equipped volunteers to "move quickly to any crisis area to prevent a breach of the peace, to assist in a cease-fire, to interpose between fighting forces, or to re-establish local law and order in case of a breakdown."
3. A U.N. Reserve Fund to finance such activities.
4. A U.N. Peace Force of twenty-five thousand, made up of "specially trained national contingents from states other than the permanent members of the Security Council" to back up the "fire brigade" in a major crisis area.
5. A supplementary force of fifty thousand composed of earmarked contingents, to be made available on two to eight weeks' notice.[13]

These essentially were modest proposals—but extremely important ones for establishing the legitimacy and efficacy of U.N. capacities for crisis intervention. They were repeatedly endorsed throughout the 1970s and 1980s by foreign policy professionals and authoritative scholars in the field of international organization. But those two decades were, for the most part, years of U.N.-discounting and even U.N.-bashing by American administrations. Perhaps the lowest point of U.S. disdain for the United Nations came when the official representative of the Reagan Administration sarcastically invited U.N. members to get out of New York and sail away into the sunset, with the U.S. delegation at the docks happily bidding them all farewell. It was a virtual echo of the John Birch Society's campaign of the 1960s: "Get the U.S. out of the U.N. and the U.N. out of the U.S.!"

In short, there was no energetic or sustained leadership from the United States government in recent decades to develop the crisis intervention and peacekeeping instruments of the United Nations. When the Persian Gulf crisis escalated in 1990, the United Nations could only respond in ad hoc fashion, which meant deferring to the military resources of the United States, virtually unilateral decision-making by the U.S. president, and military command by an American general. So the heavy irony is that U.S. neglect of the United Nations was converted into a U.N. license for the unleashing of American forces to conduct another devastating war in the Middle East.

Signals and Messages

The onset of the Persian Gulf War seems to have been a classic case of missed and misread signals, perhaps because of a more fundamental cross-cultural misunderstanding. We believe that neither the United States nor Kuwait seriously anticipated an Iraqi invasion until the last hours before it happened. On the other side, Iraq invaded Kuwait apparently without any serious anticipation of a massive military response by the United States. Intelligence and communication gaps must therefore be reckoned among the immediate causes of the war.

Throughout early 1990, however, there was increasing U.S. apprehension about a possible Iraqi threat to Israel. The Iraqi officials' February complaint to former U.S. Assistant Secretary of State Richard Murphy that Israel was planning an attack on Iraqi weapons plants was followed in March and early April by a series of incidents in Iraq-Israel relations: Iraq's trial and execution of an alleged Israeli spy (Farzad Bazoft, an Iranian-born journalist for the *London Observer*); Israel's assassination of a Canadian missile expert working for Iraq (Gerald Bull); the CIA's detection of launchers for Scud missiles in western Iraq within range of Israel; and Saddam Hussein's threat to retaliate with chemical weapons if Israel should attack first.

This preoccupation with the assumed threat of an Israeli attack was a main theme in Saddam's remarks to a visiting group of five U.S. Senators on April 12. In retrospect, that visit may have increased the possibility of an Iraqi attack on Kuwait for two reasons: by satisfying Saddam that U.S. leaders were indeed preoccupied with Israel's security and disinclined to expect an attack on Kuwait and other Gulf states; and by the reassurances given Saddam by the Senators (and on behalf of President Bush) that the United States wished to improve relations with Iraq, thereby tempting Saddam to believe the United States would not take strong action against an invasion of Kuwait. Senator Alan Simpson of Wyoming made a special effort to discount any differences between Baghdad and Washington: "I believe that your problems lie with the Western media and not with the U.S. government."

In May and June, the indignant rhetoric of Saddam Hussein and his aides over oil prices and border disputes did not seriously alter official American perceptions of Iraq's intentions, nor did it dissuade the Bush Administration from reaffirming its "normal" ties with Iraq. Saddam may indeed have used his threats against Israel as a deliberate diversion of U.S. attention from Kuwait; we may never know.

In late July, U.S. spy satellites detected the buildup of 100,000 Iraqi troops on the Kuwaiti border. Precisely because Iraq made no effort to conceal that move, the general assumption in Washington was that the buildup was a deliberately conspicuous effort to intimidate Kuwait over the oil and border disputes, not a prelude to invasion.

On July 24 in Baghdad, Egyptian President Hosni Mubarak was personally assured (and persuaded) by Saddam Hussein that Iraq had "no intention" of invading Kuwait. On the same day in Washington, State Department spokeswoman Margaret Tutwiler confidently asserted that "Iraq and others know that there is no place for coercion and intimidation in a civilized world." She added: "We do not have any defense treaties with Kuwait and there are no special defense or security commitments to Kuwait."

Back in Baghdad the next day, July 25, 1990, U.S. Ambassador April Glaspie met with Saddam Hussein in the most publicized U.S.-Iraqi diplomatic event of the entire Gulf crisis. Iraq released a partial transcript of the meeting, attributing to Glaspie a sentence which may well have indicated to Saddam that the United States would not intervene militarily should he invade Kuwait. It was a sentence that neither Glaspie nor any other U.S. official has ever contradicted: "We have no opinion on the Arab-Arab conflicts, like your border disagreement with Kuwait."

The actual invasion on August 2, and the swift occupation of the whole of Kuwait, clearly stunned the

U.S. government. Ambassador Glaspie was recalled to intramural work at the State Department and concealed from public notice for the next seven months, until three weeks after the provisional ceasefire. On March 20, 1991, she went before the Senate Foreign Relations Committee to offer her account of her July 25 meeting with Saddam. She acknowledged the accuracy of the quotation in the Iraqi transcript, but insisted that the transcript omitted her strong warnings that the United States would support its "vital interests" in the Gulf and that it therefore amounted to a "fabrication." Glaspie denied a U.S. "intelligence failure," pointing to ample evidence of Iraqi troop movements. However, she used the word "intelligence" in a very narrow sense, for she admitted that the invasion itself was not really expected: "We didn't understand Saddam Hussein," she said. "We foolishly did not realize he was stupid."

Ambassador Glaspie's testimony was about as blunt as could be: foolishness on one side, stupidity on the other, and terribly costly misjudgments on both. On the U.S. side, the misjudgments seemed to be a combination of too small a circle of top decision-makers, preoccupations with the Soviet Union and Europe and the special alignment with Israel, and the lack of significant communication with Iraqi elites and citizens.

The moral burdens of history can never be measured with exactness. There can be no doubt, however, that the United States-Iran-Iraq triangle, the unrestrained consumption of oil, the disparagement of the United Nations' security role, and the one-sided relationship with Israel all contributed significantly to the onset of the 1990 crisis in the Gulf. That history is more than enough to demonstrate that the U.S. case for a *just cause* is steeped in moral ambiguities.

Even so, the United States and other nations in the

spring and early summer of 1990 might have prevented the crisis from leading to aggression and a wider war, but for those missed and misread signals and misconceived messages.

4

Just Intent?
War Aims in the Gulf

On August 8, 1990, six days after Iraq's invasion of Kuwait, President George Bush addressed the nation from the Oval Office and announced the deployment of U.S. troops to Saudi Arabia. His address offered the first of many declarations about U.S. motives and intentions in the Gulf. He said: "I want to be clear about what we are doing and why."

The president's first words rang with a fervent appeal to the moral character and identity of the American people:

> In the life of a nation, we're called upon to define who we are and what we believe. Sometimes, these choices are not easy. But today, as president, I ask for your support in a decision I've made to stand up for what's right and condemn what's wrong, all in the cause of peace.

Specifically, the president explained, "I took this action to assist the Saudi Arabian government in the defense of its homeland." Several paragraphs later, he added the rationale of *deterrence:* "U.S. forces will work together with those of Saudi Arabia and other nations to preserve the integrity of Saudi Arabia and to deter further Iraqi aggression."

In between these appeals to defense and deterrence, the same address offered a different and more far-reaching rationale. Bush said:

> Four simple principles guide our policy:
>
> First, we seek the immediate, unconditional and complete withdrawal of all Iraqi forces from Kuwait.
>
> Second, Kuwait's legitimate government must be restored to replace the puppet regime.
>
> And third, my administration, as has been the case with every president from President Roosevelt to President Reagan, is committed to the security and stability of the Persian Gulf.
>
> And fourth, I am determined to protect the lives of American citizens abroad.

Two other passages in that August 8 address reinforced the idealistic tenor of Mr. Bush's rationale:

> America does not seek conflict, nor do we seek to chart the destiny of other nations. But America will stand by her friends. The mission of our troops is wholly defensive. Hopefully, they will not be needed long. They will not initiate hostilities. . . .
>
> Standing up for our principles is an American tradition. As it has so many times before, it may take time and tremendous effort, but most of all it will take unity of purpose. As I've witnessed throughout my life in both war and peace, America has never wavered when her purpose is driven by principle, and on this August day, at home and abroad, I know she will do no less. Thank you, and God bless the United States of America.

After escalating U.S. policy from a defensive to an offensive posture on November 8, 1990, and then launching the air war against Iraq on January 16, 1991, Mr. Bush continued to claim the traditional

principle of just intention. This appeal was made perhaps most unambiguously to the National Religious
Broadcasters Convention on January 28: "Every
war—every war—is fought for a reason. But a just
war is fought for the right reasons—for moral, not
selfish reasons." That was the address in which, as we
noted previously, the president asserted: "Our cause
could not be more noble. . . . We seek nothing for
ourselves." And he declared that "America has always been a religious nation—perhaps never more
than now," noting the "record attendance" at services
in churches, synagogues, and mosques to offer prayers
for peace during the twelve days following his initiation of the air war.

On March 6, 1991, President Bush addressed a
joint session of Congress to announce that "Aggression is defeated. The war is over." It was, he said, a
war in which "there were clear-cut objectives." It was
a war that enabled the United Nations "to fulfill the
historic vision of its founders."

> Now we can see a new world coming into view. A
> world in which there is the very real prospect of a new
> world order. . . . A world in which freedom and re-
> spect for human rights find a home among all nations.

In his March 6 peroration, Mr. Bush declared:

> We went halfway around the world to do what is moral
> and just and right. We fought hard and, with others, we
> won the war. We lifted the yoke of aggression and tyr-
> anny from a small country that many Americans had
> never even heard of, and we ask nothing in return.

This exposition of President Bush's rhetoric of
righteous intentions is, admittedly and deliberately,
quite selective. What it does not reveal is the extent to
which Mr. Bush also rationalized the war in terms of
national self-interest, even in the very same speeches.
The nobility of a just cause and just intentions may

thereby seem tarnished by grosser motives. Accordingly, these invocations of "the cause of peace," a "wholly defensive" policy, "moral, not selfish reasons," and assurances that "we seek nothing for ourselves" and "we ask nothing in return" must be weighed with at least a provisional skepticism.

In the five months between Bush's decision to deploy U.S. forces to the Gulf and the launching of the air war, the Roman Catholic bishops of the United States repeatedly communicated to government officials the bishops' concerns about the actual purposes of U.S. policy. On November 7, Archbishop Roger Mahony of Los Angeles (he has since been elevated to Cardinal), who is also chairman of the International Policy Committee of the U.S. Catholic Conference, addressed a letter to Secretary of State James Baker III that raised the most stringent questions posed by just war theory. Noting the variety of policy objectives already put forth by government leaders, Mahony insisted that the United States was still obliged "to clarify its precise objectives" and "measure them by ethical values." Citing the principle of *right intention,* he asked: "Are the reasons set forth as a just cause for war the actual objectives of military action?" Five days later, the Catholic bishops collectively adopted the Mahony letter as their own.

Discerning the true intention or motive—or mixed intentions and motives—for waging a war can be a difficult exercise in historical research and moral judgment. A decision for war, like many other political acts, can involve a whole fruit cocktail of aims and expectations. Whatever the initial intent, the momentum of military action itself can escalate and multiply the aims of war—or diminish them, if the action is frustrated or costly beyond expectations.

Searching out the war's intentions requires a critical analysis of the public rhetoric of political and military leaders. Such an analysis may disclose considerable variety, confusion, and even contradiction concerning war aims, as an examination of the Gulf War reveals.

Moreover, an assessment of the actual conduct of a war may disclose significant gaps between official rhetoric and operational objectives.

Perhaps most problematical is awaiting the revelations of historians, biographers, and memoirists who, years after the event, may uncover motives and purposes that significantly alter our understanding as to why the war was waged.

The authors confess that we do not yet know all we should like to know about U.S. war aims in the Gulf. However, we are struck by the extraordinary diversity, sometimes amounting to apparent contradictions, in the rationales offered for this war.

This difficulty was foretold by a statement from the Executive Committee of the National Council of Churches on September 14, just five weeks after Bush's deployment to Saudi Arabia. Pleading for a public debate over "the open-ended" commitment of troops and "the long-term intentions of the US with regard to a permanent military presence in the Gulf," the NCC leaders added:

> We are further concerned about the lack of clarity regarding the goals of this deployment of forces. Is the goal the restoration of the *status quo ante bellum?* Will U.S. intervention assure the return of the ruling family to power in Kuwait? Will the U.S. seek to guarantee the Kuwaitis' right to self-determination and representative government? Or is the goal of this military action preeminently the protection of U.S. access to oil supplies?[1]

Two months later, on November 15, the NCC General Board reiterated this concern, charging that the president and his aides had "done little" to clarify U.S. policy intentions. "Indeed, the rationales offered for the steady expansion of U.S. presence have often been misleading and sometimes even contradictory." The early statements about the defense of Saudi Arabia and the enforcement of U.N. sanctions had been

> supplanted by suggestions of broader goals, including expulsion of Iraqi forces from Kuwait by military means, or even offensive action against Iraq itself. The nation still has not been told in clear and certain terms what would be required for the withdrawal of U.S. troops.[2]

These concerns proved to be well-founded anticipations of the escalation of policy intentions and eventually of war aims. Still prior to Bush's initiation of the air war on January 16, historian Arthur Schlesinger, Jr., noted in *The Wall Street Journal* of January 7:

> The administration's trumpet gives an awfully uncertain sound. It has offered a rolling series of peripheral justifications—oil, jobs, regional stability, the menace of a nuclear war, the creation of a new world order. These pretexts for war grow increasingly thin.[3]

Shortly after the air war began, Elizabeth Drew similarly observed in *The New Yorker:*

> Long after the war with Iraq is over, long into the future, people will be going over and over the story, trying to figure out how we got into this war, and whether it was necessary. The extent to which the latter question will be studied will depend on things that can't be known now. . . . Of course, the president's issue with Saddam Hussein has never been simply about Kuwait. Over the months, Bush has told us that it's also about oil, about Iraq's possession of chemical weapons and the effort to achieve a nuclear weapon, about the threat Hussein poses to his other neighbors, and about the need to establish a "new world order" . . . .[4]

These observations by outsiders were reinforced by some insiders, notably General Colin Powell, Chairman of the Joint Chiefs of Staff. Powell, of all people, did not know how or just when Bush decided to deploy troops to Saudi Arabia. There had been no policy papers laying out the alternatives, or the decision itself, or the implications. Nor had there been any clear statement about goals in the first several days after the deployment decision.[5]

A more systematic inquiry into policy intentions is clearly called for, but it can hardly be completed at present or within this limited case study. Some additional reflections, however, may be structured by the following list of articulated or speculated objectives:

1. A "new world order" of collective security against aggression
2. A Pax Americana in the Middle East
3. The protection of oil interests
4. The destruction of Iraq's chemical and nuclear weapons capabilities
5. The defeat of Israel's prime adversary
6. The personal and political motives of George Bush

1. *New World Order*

The visionary rhetoric of a new world order is very old; as old as Isaiah and Cicero and Grotius and Kant and Woodrow Wilson. During World War II, American churches fervently campaigned for a stronger postwar United Nations; their basic themes were a "new world order" and a "just and durable peace." The largest mainline denomination, the Methodist Church, launched its "Crusade for a New World Order" in 1943.

On August 23, 1990, two weeks after the deployment of U.S. forces to Saudi Arabia, President Bush's

National Security Adviser, Brent Scowcroft, reported that he and the president had held a "searching discussion" concerning "the broader ramifications of what we were doing and what it might mean." That four-hour discussion took place on a fishing expedition near Kennebunkport, Maine. The catch: three bluefish and a rhetorical catchword for administration policy, "new world order." Later that day, Scowcroft explained the latter catch: "We believe we are creating the beginning of a new world order coming out of the collapse of the US-Soviet antagonisms. . . . We're trying to build an order beyond this crisis." A scrutiny of presidential documents reveals that Mr. Bush's public orations between August 1990 and March 1991 included at least forty-two invocations of a "new world order."[6]

Again and again, Bush, his aides, and the media characterized the Gulf crisis as "the defining moment for a new world order." Even the National Council of Churches picked up on the phrase in its November 15 resolution:

> We stand on the threshold of a "new world order." Indeed, the near unanimous condemnation by the nations of the world of Iraq's illegal occupation of its neighbor, Kuwait, shows the promise of a new approach to the vocation of peacemaking for which the United Nations was created 45 years ago. There are present in this moment seeds either of a new era of international cooperation under the rule of international law or of rule based upon superior power, which holds the prospect of continuing dehumanizing chaos.

While the "new world order" theme typically was associated with a stronger United Nations and stronger collective security against aggression, its positive content was never clearly defined during the Gulf War. Nevertheless, it served to solidify bipartisan and public support for Bush's war policies. Democratic Congressman Stephen J. Solarz of New York, a prime supporter of offensive military action against Iraq, was notably enthusiastic:

> This crisis provides a rare opportunity, perhaps the first since the dawn of the modern age, to create a world order in which the international community upholds the sanctity of existing borders and the principle that nations should not be permitted to invade and to annex their weaker neighbors.

Solarz also imagined that "the dream of Franklin Roosevelt and the other founders of the United Nations, that the world organization would be used by the great powers as a mechanism for the preservation of peace, is being realized."[7]

Henry Kissinger, for one, remained skeptical of such a dream. While professing admiration for President Bush's "skill and fortitude in building the coalition," Kissinger viewed Bush's rhetoric as an appeal to the illusions of Wilsonian idealism, with its moralistic rejection of necessary balance-of-power policies. He judged that "the new world order cannot possibly fulfill the idealistic expectations expressed by the president; I doubt indeed whether they accurately describe what happened during the Gulf crisis."[8]

Dr. Kissinger did not expand on that latter clause to suggest that the "new world order" was a fabrication of U.S. policy intentions in the Gulf, but others have so suggested. Jim Wallis, editor of the evangelical magazine *Sojourners,* in an April 1991 editorial titled "Neither Just nor Holy War: Dissenting from the New World Order," asserted that

> The credibility of the new world order of which George Bush now constantly speaks is the central issue in this war. That new world order will be enforced and controlled by the military supremacy and political direction of the United States. . . . The new order will be

financed and supported by the other rich nations who, along with the United States, will be its primary beneficiaries.[9]

Other critics measured the credibility of Bush's "new world order" by the overall performance of U.S. policies in the United Nations during the past decade: a record largely of obstruction and estrangement. We shall discuss this issue in chapter 6 in the context of the just war tradition's imperative of *legitimate authority,* given the Bush administration's appeal to U.N. Security Council resolutions as the juridical bases of U.S. policies in the Gulf.

2. *A Pax Americana in the Middle East*

It is possible to believe in the earnestness of "new world order" intentions while understanding that concept not as a genuinely multilateral concert but as an essentially unilateral projection of American power in a unipolar world after the end of the Cold War. It is also possible to doubt the primacy of "new world order" goals and to view the Gulf War as an even more blatant show of American power—as a new Pax Americana.

Thomas L. Friedman, chief diplomatic correspondent of *The New York Times,* was an early skeptic of President Bush's August 8, 1990, principled rationale for sending troops to the Gulf:

> One reason Bush administration officials have not clearly articulated what is at stake is that the real political and economic interests involved are not quite so lofty as some of the broad principles used by the president to explain the operation. The United States has not sent troops to the Saudi desert to preserve democratic principles. . . . Surely it is not American policy to make the world safe for feudalism.

Rather, the prime purpose of U.S. policy, according to Friedman, was national self-interest in "preserving the status quo and stability in the Persian Gulf."[10]

Such a purpose could draw on decades of presidential utterances, such as Franklin Roosevelt's 1943 declaration: "The defense of Saudi Arabia is vital to the defense of the United States," or President Carter's 1980 rationale for dispatching a new "Rapid Deployment Force" to the Gulf: "An attempt by any outside force to gain control of the Persian Gulf region will be regarded as an assault on the vital interests of the United States, and such an assault will be repelled by any means necessary, including military force."

Carter's notions of "outside force" focused on the Islamic fundamentalism of Iran under Ayatollah Ruhollah Khomeini (hardly an outsider to the Persian Gulf, though not an Arab power) and the presumed Soviet drive toward the Gulf, attributed to the 1979 invasion of Afghanistan. If the credibility of that presumption about Soviet intentions was always in doubt, the bitter frustration of Soviet power within Afghanistan itself made further attempts at expansion impossible.

In 1983, the Rapid Deployment Force was transformed into a separate military command: Central Command (CENTCOM), a name suggesting a relic of the defunct Central Treaty Organization (CENTO), a euphemism for what was formerly the Baghdad Pact. That Anglo-American Pact, formed in 1955 to counter Soviet influence in the Middle East, originally included Iraq, Iran, Pakistan, and Turkey. Iraq pulled out after the 1958 anti-Western coup by Abdul Karem Kassem; the headquarters of the Pact moved from Baghdad to Ankara. Iran pulled out after the Khomeini revolution of 1979, whereupon CENTO, bereft of both Iraq and Iran, was dissolved. The U.S. Central Command headquarters was moved far from the volatile Middle East to MacDill Air Force Base near Tampa, Florida. No Middle Eastern country proved willing to host the Central Command. Anti-Western and anti-Israel sentiments made all Arab rulers disinclined to become conspicuously connected with U.S. strategic interests.

Questions of motivation and intention rightly become questions of morality and character. It is a speculative and sometimes perilous exercise to attempt to judge the moral core and character of policy makers. But a truly democratic society must insist on the right to subject public leaders to moral and philosophical scrutiny concerning their purposes for the nation and its foreign policies. Christopher Hitchens, the Washington editor of *Harper's,* views George Bush as more a cynical practitioner of *realpolitik,* in the tradition of Metternich and Kissinger, than a promoter of principled internationalism, and as a former CIA director who has long been engaged in the game of "superpower divide-and-rule."[11] Hitchens' boss, *Harper's* editor Lewis Lapham, had no doubt that George Bush's motives in the Gulf were those of "the old world order, the one governed by force and the show of force."

> During the autumn advertising campaign meant to sell the American public on the prospect of war in Iraq, President Bush dressed up his gunboat diplomacy in the slogans of conscience and the costume of what he was pleased to call "the new world order." . . . The president's righteousness waxed increasingly militant as the merely political or commercial reasons for war proved inadequate to the occasion. . . . The autumn's diplomatic maneuvers make it clear that the White House meant to restore what used to be called the "Pax Americana."[12]

In his April 1991 "dissent from the new world order," Jim Wallis insisted that "the imposition of Pax
Americana" had been the ultimate purpose of the
Gulf War from the beginning. Wallis rejected the notion that a Pax Americana could offer a genuinely new
world order:

> A world dominated by one superpower, instead of two,
> is neither safer, freer, nor more just—especially for
> those on the bottom. . . . It is now abundantly clear
> that George Bush and the American power elite saw
> the end of the Cold War not as an opportunity for
> peace and new cooperation, but as the chance for sin-
> gular dominance. . . . a new world order made safe
> only by the continued ability of the United States to
> inflict massive violence on "outlaw" nations. And the
> American world policeman gets to define the law.[13]

That charge of a U.S. bid for "singular dominance"
was alleged by some critics to apply not only to power
over the Soviet Union and regional states in the Middle East but over U.S. allies as well. The Pax Americana would provide an opportunity to offset the
surging economic powers of Western Europe and East
Asia. Nubar Hovsepian, professor of Middle East politics at Hunter College, opined that the United States

> will not relinquish its new-found military bases in the
> Middle East in the foreseeable future. They not only
> secure America's desire for hegemonic control of the
> region, but provide the U.S. with the needed leverage
> over its European and Japanese allies. After all, the
> U.S. is quite worried about its economic competitive-
> ness with the Europe of 1992.[14]

Whatever the truth about White House intentions
concerning U.S. allies, heavy administration pressures on Germany and Japan to provide multi–billion
dollar subsidies of U.S. forces and to play a more ac-
tive political and military role in the Gulf War clearly

strained alliance relationships, as did U.S.-French
differences over policy objectives.

The new-found military bases to which Hovsepian
referred had their origins in a developing *de facto* U.S.
alliance with the Saudi Monarchy that began in the
1970s. During that decade Saudi Arabia bought more
than $3 billion worth of U.S. arms and equipment,
and hosted hundreds of U.S. military advisers and ten
thousand U.S. civilians who were there to help build
Saudi military bases. In the early 1980s, the United
States sold five AWACS (airborne warning and control
planes) to Saudi Arabia; the Saudis spent $50 billion
on an extensive air defense system compatible with
U.S. military requirements; and more military bases,
military schools and training centers, headquarters
complexes, and port facilities were constructed in
Saudi Arabia, largely under the direction of the U.S.
Army's Corps of Engineers.[15]

Operation Desert Storm thus was launched from a
thoroughly Americanized military network in Saudi
Arabia. It was not a pristine projection of U.S. forces
"over there."

Michael Klare, defense correspondent for *The Nation,* describes Operation Desert Storm as "the new
paradigm for US military action in the 1990s." That
paradigm embodies a high-tech, high-speed use of the
most sophisticated military technologies, as well as a
new concept of "mid-intensity conflict" (MIC) in
Third World regions, in contrast with "high-intensity
combat" in Europe and "low-intensity combat" (LIC)
in Central America. In September of 1990, four
months before the launching of Desert Storm, General Norman Schwarzkopf hinted at the style of strategic planning in which the United States was then
engaged: "We would be using capabilities that are far
more lethal, far more accurate, and far more effective
than anything we've ever used."[16]

3. *Oil*

Both "new world order" and "Pax Americana" are, after all, rather abstract concepts that can obscure concrete intentions. Clearly the most concrete intention of U.S. policy in the Persian Gulf has been the protection of oil interests from domination by any nation hostile to the United States or to oil-rich Saudi Arabia and the smaller Gulf states. In anticipation of such a conflict, Ronald Reagan's Secretary of Defense Caspar Weinberger, in a classified 1984–88 Defense Guidance report, wrote that the United States "should be prepared to introduce American forces directly into the region should it appear that the security of access to Persian Gulf oil is threatened."[17]

Although President Bush's "four simple principles" set forth on August 8, 1990, made no specific mention of oil, Bush explained later in the same speech that "the stakes are high. . . . Our country now imports nearly half the oil it consumes and could face a major threat to its economic independence." That statement is notable not only for its separation from the president's "principles" but also for characterizing U.S. oil *dependence* as "independence."

A week later, in an address on August 15 at the Pentagon, Bush was even more candid about U.S. self-interests in the Gulf. This was the oft-quoted speech in which he asserted that "our way of life" was at stake:

> Our action in the Gulf . . . is about our national security interests and . . . about maintaining access to energy resources that are key not just to the functioning of this country, but to the entire world. Our jobs, our way of life, our own freedom and the freedom of friendly countries around the world would all suffer if control of the world's great oil reserves fell into the hands of that one man, Saddam Hussein.

Indeed, the Persian Gulf region contains more than two-thirds of the world's known oil reserves.

Up to 1990 the U.S. government had been unwilling to adopt the energy policies that would make the nation less driven to a war for oil. In addition to a much more resolute priority on alternative energy sources, such policies would have to include the following: conservation measures such as gas taxes at the pump and requirements for more fuel-efficient cars; an increase in the production of domestic oil, the high cost of which could be offset by surcharges on oil imports; and tax rebates and reduced surcharges for farmers, low-income groups, and others likely to be disproportionately affected by more stringent oil policies.

The political and moral reality for Americans in recent years has been that it is easier to go to war for oil than to adopt energy policies that even to a minimal degree may inhibit "our way of life." In fact, Bush's own 1991 energy plan points mostly in the opposite direction: deregulation without taxation. For example, the plan would abolish the U.S. government ban on oil drilling in Alaska's Arctic National Wildlife Refuge. That is one more policy typical of the licentious 1980s: to promote private interests and to avoid public discipline.

The New York Times's Thomas Friedman had no doubt as to why Bush deployed forces to Saudi Arabia: "Laid bare, American policy in the Gulf comes down to this: Troops have been sent to retain control of oil in the hands of a pro-American Saudi Arabia, so prices will remain low." Friedman suggests the war was fought "to make the world safe for gas guzzlers." An editorial cartoon in *The Boston Globe* portrays President Bush in the Oval Office addressing the American people. He is saying:

> Fellow Americans, I have sent our troops to the Middle East. . . . They are there to defend the security . . . the

value . . . the principle we hold dear—18 miles per gallon.[18]

We suspect that is an oversimplification of Bush's intentions. Moreover, the intention to keep such a despot as Saddam Hussein from aggressive seizure of oil interests on which many nations depend is certainly a legitimate ethical concern. What is just as certain, however, is that Bush's moral pretenses were never credibly connected with oil interests and that U.S. energy policies in the 1980s contributed greatly to the onset of the Gulf crisis.

4. *Iraq's chemical and nuclear weapons*

Before August 1990, the U.S. government declined to take any decisive action against Iraq for its chemical weapons and warfare or for its presumed drive to develop nuclear weapons. From August 2, 1990, until January 16, 1991, as U.S. policy aims in the Gulf escalated from the "wholly defensive" to an "offensive military option" to the launching of the air war, a growing chorus demanded the outright destruction of Iraq's unconventional weapons. In November, President Bush and his aides publicly announced that the United States might have to go to war to prevent Iraq's production of nuclear weapons, said to be possible within six months to a year.

This sudden alarmism about Iraq's nuclear potential came in the face of widespread expert consensus in the United States and abroad that Iraq, if bent on developing nuclear weapons, would require five to ten years to do so. But George Bush, in Saudi Arabia on Thanksgiving Day, informed an audience of U.S. troops (and the world) that "Every day that passes brings Saddam Hussein one step closer to realizing his goal of a nuclear weapons arsenal—and that's another reason, frankly, why our mission is marked by a real

sense of urgency." Thus the aims of a war to be
launched six weeks later stretched far beyond the defense of Saudi Arabia.

The joint congressional resolution of January 12,
1991, made it official: The use of U.S. armed forces
could be authorized by the president in view of
"Iraq's conventional, chemical, biological, and nuclear weapons and ballistic missile programs" that
"pose[d] a grave threat to world peace." Four days
later, in announcing the launching of the air war,
George Bush declared: "We are determined to knock
out Saddam Hussein's nuclear bomb potential. We
will also destroy his chemical weapons facilities."

Officially, Iraq is a party to the Nuclear Non-Prolif-
eration Treaty, and its nuclear facilities have been
subject to inspection by the International Atomic Energy Agency. While Saddam Hussein had imported
nuclear materials and related technologies from the
United States, Germany, Switzerland, Brazil, and
China, and was widely believed to have nuclear weapons ambitions, nothing in the IAEA inspections or in
the twelve U.N. Security Council resolutions on Iraq
specifically warranted the destruction of its "nuclear
bomb potential." However, it was disclosed in July of
1991 that Iraq had concealed from the IAEA a "low
tech" method of uranium enrichment (electromagne-
tism through machines called calutrons) that perhaps
was capable of eventually producing one or more nuclear weapons. That concealment exposed both the
unending treachery of Saddam Hussein and the limited efficacy of the world's nonproliferation regime,
vested largely in the IAEA. But even an Iraqi threat to
use a "crude" nuclear weapon against Israel would
surely have been suicidal, given Israel's undoubted
nuclear arsenal.

The nuclear rationale for the war against Iraq, coming as it did in November at a time of precarious public support for Bush's increasingly offense-minded

policies, remains somewhat suspect; it was perhaps a case of rhetorical excess. A mid-November opinion poll, published in *USA Today* under the headline "Bush Support Slim," reported that public approval of Bush's handling of the Gulf crisis had tumbled from 82 to 51 percent since August. The nuclear alarm, followed on November 30 by Bush's first offer of talks with Baghdad, clearly recouped much public support.

However, even the long-range specter of a nuclear rival to nuclear-capable Israel was, along with Saddam Hussein's threats to retaliate against Israel with chemical weapons, undoubtedly intolerable to many U.S. and Israeli officials. There was unquestionably an Israeli dimension to U.S. intentions in the Gulf crisis.

5. *A War for Israel?*

On January 16, 1991, the day Bush's air assault on Iraq began, C. William Maynes, editor of *Foreign Policy* and former Assistant Secretary of State in the Carter administration, wrote: "When historians examine the reasons behind the U.S. decision to go to war in the Persian Gulf on this day, they are likely to identify four: oil, order, security, and Israel." By listing Israel fourth and last among the reasons for war, Maynes did not suggest that Israel was the least important factor. However, the covert aspects of the U.S.-Israel alliance and of Israel's own military policies make the ferreting out of U.S. intentions concerning Israel particularly difficult. Maynes noted that many pro-Israel groups in the U.S. had viewed the Gulf crisis as an opportunity to bolster Israel's security. They opposed economic sanctions because sanctions would not accomplish the total destruction of Saddam Hussein's military machine, regarded as the greatest threat to the security of Israel. The editors of both *Commen-*

tary and *Tikkun,* prominent Jewish journals (the former conservative, the latter liberal), advocated a
resort to war to destroy Iraq as a military force in the
Middle East. That was also claimed by Capitol Hill
insiders to be the main motive behind Congressman
Solarz's enthusiastic "new world order" rhetoric.
When an ecumenical deputation of Christian leaders
met with Bush to urge an antiwar policy, the American Jewish Committee accused them of playing "directly into the hands of Saddam Hussein."[19] As the
crisis escalated, strenuous efforts to formulate a common Christian-Jewish stance against war broke down.
    Many Jews in both the United States and Israel
have shared the conviction of A. M. Rosenthal, former executive editor of *The New York Times,* that
Saddam Hussein's "vision of ultimate duty and des-
tiny" is the elimination of the state of Israel. Saddam's April 2, 1990, threat to burn half of Israel
(albeit in retaliation for any preemptive Israeli attack
on Iraq), and his repeated charges of a Zionist plot
against Iraq, intensified that conviction. Before the
Congressional votes of January 12, 1991, on the use-
of-force resolutions, the hard-line American Israel
Public Affairs Committee (AIPAC) worked closely
with the White House to lobby support for the resolutions.
    These happenings do not necessarily settle the ques-
tion as to what intentions occupied the mind of
George Bush in going to war. Some Western journalists (such as Milton Viorst in *The New Yorker* and
John Pilger in the British weekly *New Statesman and
Nation*) have speculated that the United States deliberately lured Iraq into a war so that Saddam Hussein
could be eliminated as a threat to Israel and to U.S.
interests in the Gulf. We have yet to find persuasive
evidence of such a design. To date, there seems to be
more persuasive evidence that the United States, Kuwait, Saudi Arabia, Egypt, Jordan, and other govern-

ments were genuinely surprised by the invasion of Kuwait—in short, that the intelligence failures were real.

Nevertheless, James M. Wall, editor of *The Christian Century* and a veteran pundit on Middle East affairs, has imagined that George Bush "intended from the outset to eliminate Saddam Hussein for the sake of Israel's security and American oil interests." On this view, Bush may have been responding "as much to the Arab summit meeting of May 1990 as he was to the Iraqi invasion."[20] That was the summit at which Yasir Arafat sought unified Arab action against Jewish settlements on the West Bank and at which a resolution sharply condemned the United States for its political, economic, and military support of Israel. To suppose that Bush went to war for the sake of Israel is not necessarily to subscribe to the theory that he lured Saddam into war at Israel's behest, but it may suggest that after Iraq's invasion of Kuwait, Bush's decision for war could well have been conditioned by Israel's desire to destroy Saddam's military threat.

The Israeli factor in Bush's policies is indeed a subject for historians to investigate in times to come.

6. *Personal and political*

The most elusive of policy intentions may be those that lie within the inner recesses of character and personality. There may never be a full or final accounting as to why George Bush committed the United States to a war against Iraq. However, both close associates of the president and outside observers have portrayed him as personally obsessed with Saddam Hussein, to the virtual exclusion of other responsibilities—perhaps partly because of a sense of personal betrayal after years of pro-Iraq policies in the 1980s. Some analysts came to believe that Bush really committed himself to war in the very first days, if not hours, after

Iraq's invasion of Kuwait. Speaking positively, some public figures and president-watchers approvingly declared that they had never seen George Bush more focused and more resolute than he had been from August to January.

By all accounts, Bush permitted only a tiny circle of aides—perhaps as few as seven or eight—to be privy to his decision-making, and even "principals" in that circle often felt left out in the cold. Interviews with both Pentagon and State Department officials testify that almost everybody with Middle East policy expertise was excluded. Not until January 8, 1991, a week before launching the air war, did Bush first meet with April Glaspie, U.S. ambassador to Iraq, and several other specialists in Arab affairs.

Bob Woodward's book *The Commanders* portrays the private, off-the-record Bush as very different from his usually thoughtful, well-tempered public persona. Woodward reports the testimony of Secretary of Defense Dick Cheney that Bush "has got a long history of vindictive political actions. Cross Bush and you pay."[21] Joint Chiefs Chairman Colin Powell says Bush's very emotional decision to escalate war aims in the Gulf (a decision from which Powell was excluded) was like a cowboy firing away with "six shooters in both hands."[22] In fact, Powell recalled that "there had been no debate on whether to make the deployment" of U.S. forces to Saudi Arabia; it was Bush's personal decision. Powell's predecessor, Admiral William Crowe, according to Woodward "a skeptic about all uses of force," worried that presidents sometimes had "ambitions, extravagant ideas about the goals they could achieve with military power." When Bush determined that the military should intervene in Panama to seize strongman Manuel Noriega, Crowe "saw no signs that the consequences were being fully considered."[23] The civilian leaders of the Bush administration, particularly Bush himself and Secretary Cheney, were clearly more hawkish than the military commanders. Powell's efforts to advise diplomatic solutions and protracted sanctions against Iraq never had a chance, given the inhibiting dynamics of Bush's inner circle, according to Woodward.[24]

This picture of the president as impetuous, impatient with nonmilitary options, and directing a devious and intimidating decision-making process camouflaged with highly principled public rhetoric, does not by itself explain Bush's intentions—even if the picture is true.

Were there domestic political motives? In the early months of the Bush administration, Admiral Crowe observed that security policy was shaped more by political calculations than by military and foreign policy criteria. Decisions taken at National Security Council (NSC) meetings were based on "their likely impact on the Congress, the media, and public opinion, and the focus was on managing the reaction."[25] With regard to Iraq, Bush's chief of staff, John Sununu, informed associates that "a short, successful war would be pure political gold for the president—would guarantee his reelection." Some observers believed that Bush decided to "bring things to a head in January" because he "didn't want to risk a protracted war in an election year."[26] Whatever Bush's motives, his public support, according to opinion polls, skyrocketed to the 90 percent level in the wake of the swift U.S. military victory over Iraq. In fact, so solid seemed Bush's reelection prospects in the summer of 1991 that a parade of potential Democratic presidential candidates renounced their availability for 1992.

A more intimate view of Bush's personal investment in Operation Desert Storm emphasized his presumed need to overcome the "wimp factor": to prove to himself and to the world that his presidency, hitherto unfocused (especially with regard to domestic issues), had obscured what a tough guy he really is. A senator, with much reluctance, told Elizabeth Drew:

> We all know instinctively [that Bush] is not a strong man. It's greatly disturbing. I try not to think about it. I don't know anyone who's honest with himself who doesn't think this.

Drew herself observed that Bush's personalizing of his conflict with Saddam Hussein, "when he swaggered and did his Clint Eastwood routine, when he said that Hussein is 'going to get his ass kicked,' " made more credible the notion that he was trying to prove his manhood.[27]

Mixed Fruit and Moral Dualism

This review of the norm of *just intention,* as applied to U.S. war aims in the Gulf, has featured public rhetoric, in its appeals to both moral principles and self-interests, and not-so-public factors that may have played a part in decision-making by George Bush and his aides. Much of the review remains speculative. It is unlikely that the decision for war can ever be pinned to a single intention. Thus, we repeat: A whole fruit cocktail of aims and expectations may well have determined the resort to Operation Desert Storm. And we note that the mixture of lofty moralism and macho self-interest in this case is hardly new in American experience. It is one more incarnation of the moral dualism that seems to have been with us from the founding of our republic.

5

Last Resort?
The Miles of Peace

The just war tradition's presumption against the resort to war, unless all reasonable approaches to a just
and peaceful settlement have been tried and have
failed, emerged as the central focus of a vigorous debate in the weeks before January 15, 1991. That debate sharply divided Congress and nearly denied
congressional approval of presidential authority to
wage war against Iraq. The debate found the nation's
most eminent military leaders, veteran diplomats,
and academic experts at odds with one another in
what was, at least for a few weeks between mid-
November, 1990, and mid-January, 1991, perhaps
the most extraordinary controversy ever staged
within the national security establishment. Primarily
at issue were the efficacy of economic sanctions and
the feasibility of diplomatic negotiations. However,
this was mostly an arcane Washington controversy
that failed to engage the general public until the final
three-day congressional debate in January.

The Joint Congressional Resolution of January 12,
1991, authorized the president's use of the Armed
Forces, should he determine that "the United States

has used all appropriate diplomatic and other peaceful means to obtain compliance by Iraq" with the twelve U.N. Security Council resolutions.

On January 16, President Bush, in announcing the air attacks on "military targets in Iraq and Kuwait," invoked both the U.N. and congressional resolutions in support of the principle of *last resort*. He said:

> This military action . . . follows months of constant and virtually endless diplomatic activity on the part of the United Nations, the United States and many, many other countries. . . . The world could wait no longer. Sanctions, though having some effect, showed no signs of accomplishing their objective. . . . The United States, together with the United Nations, exhausted every means at our disposal to bring this crisis to a peaceful end.

Speaking to the National Religious Broadcasters twelve days later, Bush was more explicit, even statistical:

> A just war must be a last resort. . . . We tried to resolve this conflict. Secretary of State Jim Baker made an extraordinary effort to achieve peace. More than two hundred meetings with foreign dignitaries, ten diplomatic missions, six congressional appearances. Over 103,000 miles traveled. . . . And sadly, Saddam Hussein rejected out of hand every overture. . . . He made this just war an inevitable war.

The Administration and Sanctions

Back in August and September of 1990, when Bush was articulating a strictly defensive military policy, he expressed strong and optimistic support for the economic sanctions approved by the U.N. Security Council under Chapter VII of the U.N. Charter. He told the nation on August 8:

These sanctions, now enshrined in international law, have the potential to deny Iraq the fruits of aggression, while sharply limiting its ability to either import or export anything of value, especially oil. I pledge here today that the United States will do its part to see that these sanctions are effective and to induce Iraq to withdraw, without delay, from Kuwait.

A week later at the Pentagon, Bush reported that Iraq had been cut off from most of the world. "Sanctions are working. . . . And ships of numerous countries are sailing with ours to see that UN sanctions . . . are enforced." Speaking to a joint session of Congress on September 11, Bush gave a rousing progress report on sanctions, while urging patience over the protracted time required for sanctions to achieve their objective: Iraq's withdrawal from Kuwait.

Let no one doubt our staying power. . . . Together with our friends and allies, ships of the United States Navy are today patrolling Mideast waters. They've already intercepted more than 700 ships to enforce the sanctions. . . . Iraq is feeling the heat. . . . They are cut off from world trade, unable to sell their oil. And only a tiny fraction of goods get through. . . . Sanctions will take time to have their full intended effect.

As late as December 5, CIA Director William H. Webster told the House Armed Services Committee that "more than 90 percent of imports and 97 percent of exports have been shut off." By next spring, "probably only energy-related and some military industries will be fully functioning."

At the very heart of the history of the Gulf war is the question as to why George Bush then abandoned his announced strategy of a "wholly defensive" military deployment, combined with economic sanctions that he and CIA Director Webster claimed to be extremely effective. That is a question still shrouded in secrecy and propaganda. Bob Woodward's case study *The Commanders* does not address the question directly. Since even some of the "principals" in Bush's inner circle seem uncertain about the answer, as we have seen, historians will have to dig very deeply to find it.

One way of reading Bush's reversal on the effectiveness of sanctions is to suggest that his escalating objectives in the crisis rose above and beyond the capacity of sanctions to achieve them. The defense of Saudi Arabia and Iraq's withdrawal from Kuwait were no doubt more amenable to sanctions than were the more ambitious goals of destroying Iraq's chemical and nuclear powers, or decimating Saddam Hussein's army, or overthrowing his regime.

It has also been widely suggested that Bush moved precipitately toward an offensive war for one or more reasons of timing: the logistical and psychological difficulties of sustaining a huge army in the desert over a period of many months; the need to fight a war before Islam's holy month of fasting, Ramadan (which literally means "the hot month"), beginning in March; and concern that the multinational coalition might disintegrate under various public and diplomatic pressures.

But if, as some Bush-watchers believed from the start, George Bush actually had made up his mind to defeat Iraq militarily in the very first days after August 2, then the sanctions and diplomatic exercises were games to be played while the warriors were being prepared for combat. Some Bush aides believed that the president's tough August rhetoric made war inevitable and that economic sanctions were the prelude to war, not an alternative to it. Elizabeth Drew reported:

> It was clear from very early on that some officials saw sanctions and diplomacy as the necessary political precursors of war—that each would be, as one official put

it, "a box to check." In the early days, an official said to me that by the time we went to war the president would be able to say that he tried sanctions and tried diplomacy. They were also the necessary logistical precursors of war: The military needed time to build up its forces in the Gulf regions.[1]

If that is really the way it was with George Bush, the claim of last resort is a pious untruth. Still, it might be said by a true believer in Pax Americana, or by some sophisticated moralist, that it was a justifiable pious untruth.

Giving Sanctions a Chance

The main intramural debate within the foreign policy establishment from mid-November of 1990 to mid-January of 1991 was over the sanctions strategy behind which Bush and Baker had rallied the U.N. coalition. When it increasingly seemed that Bush was discounting that strategy while preparing the "offensive military option," a distinguished array of members of the Senate and the House, former Secretaries of Defense, former chairmen of the Joint Chiefs of Staff, and other national security eminences rallied around the original defensive-plus-sanctions strategy. They claimed to support the president's August-to-November strategy after he himself had given every indication of forsaking his own policies.

Foremost among the military advocates of the nonmilitary approach through sanctions was Admiral William Crowe, who had served both Presidents Reagan and Bush as chairman of the Joint Chiefs of Staff. Appearing before the Senate Armed Services Committee on November 28, Crowe testified to his belief that sanctions would ultimately succeed in pushing Saddam Hussein out of Kuwait, Bush's originally announced objective. The admiral acknowledged that sanctions might take twelve to eighteen months to achieve that objective, but insisted that was a worthy "tradeoff of avoiding war, with its attendant sacrifices and uncertainties." The avoidance of hostilities and casualties, he said, should be regarded as not only "highly desirable ends," but as "national interests. I seldom hear them referred to in that fashion." Crowe concluded with a stirring appeal for national patience:

> It is curious that just as our patience in Western Europe has paid off and furnished us the most graphic example in our history of how staunchness is sometimes the better course in dealing with thorny international problems, a few armchair strategists are counseling a near-term attack on Iraq. . . . It would be a sad commentary if Saddam Hussein, a two-bit tyrant who sits on seventeen million people and possesses a gross national product of $40 billion, proved to be more patient than the United States, the world's most affluent and powerful nation.

On that same day, Crowe's JCS predecessor, General David Jones, offered similar testimony in favor of sanctions instead of war. In questioning the wisdom of Bush's escalation of force levels for an "offensive military option," Jones said his main concern "isn't that we might choose to fight but rather that the deployment might cause us to fight, perhaps prematurely and perhaps unnecessarily." Jones argued that the historical analogy for the Gulf crisis was not Munich, with its failure to resist aggression, but 1914, with its senseless stumbling into a war that should have been avoided.

Also on that same day, in the same hearing room, Henry Kissinger urged the Senate to support the resort to war and "the destruction of the Iraqi military complex." (With the end of the Cold War, Kissinger has been increasingly preoccupied with the projection of U.S. military power in the Third World.) And in

New York that day, administration representatives were rounding up votes for the next day's U.N. Security Council resolution that would authorize the resort to war.

Six former Secretaries of Defense supported prolonged sanctions instead of the early resort to war. On December 4, ex-Pentagon chief Robert McNamara declared to the Senate Foreign Relations Committee: "Surely we should be prepared to give the sanctions 12 to 18 months to work, if we wish to achieve our political objectives. . . . Who can doubt that a year of blockade would be cheaper than one week of war?"

The next day, former National Security Adviser Zbigniew Brzezinski urged the Committee to advise the administration to "stay the course" with economic sanctions. Brzezinski, with notable earnestness, declared:

> This policy is working. Iraq has been deterred, ostracized, and punished. Sanctions, unprecedented in their international solidarity and more massive in scope than any ever adopted in peacetime against any nation—I repeat, ever adopted against any nation, are inflicting painful costs on the Iraqi economy.

Brzezinski accused the Bush administration of impatience and naïveté as to how sanctions actually work. They take time, he said, but the White House rhetoric of impatience "has tended to undermine the credibility of long-term sanctions." The consequence had been to

> make the administration the prisoner of its own rhetoric, with American options and timetable thereby severely constricted. . . . The conflict of the international community with Iraq has become over-Americanized, over-personalized, and over-emotionalized. The enormous deployment of American forces, coupled with talk of no compromise, means that the United States is now

pointed toward a war with Iraq that will be largely an American war, fought predominantly by Americans . . . and for interests that are neither equally vital nor urgent to America and which, in any case, can be and should be effectively pursued by other less dramatic and less bloody means.

Diplomacy Without Negotiations?

George Bush's justification of his war against Iraq as a legitimate last resort was based not only on his downgrading of economic sanctions in the face of much contrary testimony; he insisted that there had been "months of constant and virtually endless diplomatic activity" to no avail and that "the world could wait no longer."

Those claims are rightly tested by three historical questions that cannot yet be definitively answered.

1. Was the "diplomacy" practiced by Bush and his aides actually a political and logistical precursor to war, a public relations exercise designed as a holding operation while the U.S. and U.N. Coalition forces were built up in the Gulf?
2. If the administration's "diplomacy" was really intended to provide a peaceful settlement of the Gulf crisis, did the very style of its approach tend to guarantee failure?
3. Did the United States effectively obstruct the diplomatic opportunities offered by other governments and the United Nations?

In the Gulf case, as in many others, there is some evidence that the administration was not of one mind as to how to deal with an adversary. Secretary of State Baker is reported to have believed that "there could and should be a political settlement." Some advisers thought that Bush, with his harsh terms for a settlement and his bullying rhetoric, pushed both Saddam

Hussein and himself into a corner. A former Pentagon official complained:

> You don't talk to Arabs like they're dogs in the street; you don't say you're going to kick their ass. This is not to say he would have backed down, but that level of discourse isn't conducive to a diplomatic solution.[2]

The months of August, September, and October went by without any administration proposal for direct communication between the United States and Iraq. In late October, Jimmy Carter noted this lack in a *Time* magazine article titled "The Need to Negotiate":

> So far, the Bush administration has not acknowledged the need for negotiations or exploratory talks, which might imply weakness or a willingness to reverse adamant public statements. Initiating peace talks is always difficult, as we remember from Korea and Vietnam. Only unconditional surrender following a total military victory can remove the need for negotiated settlements.

Carter went on to propose a list of "intermediaries" who might facilitate negotiations: U.N. officials, Soviet leaders, French or other allies, Arab states.

Carter's preference was that Arab diplomacy be given an opportunity to initiate peace talks. Further, he defended the capacity of Jordan's King Hussein to "play a key role," characterizing him as "an honorable and peace-loving man who does not deserve the harsh treatment he is receiving." Hussein had supported the U.N. resolutions demanding Iraq's withdrawal from Kuwait and imposing economic sanctions.[3] Those sanctions, he surely knew, would exact heavy economic costs from Jordan, given that country's dependence on Iraq for cheap oil and as a prime market for Jordan's exports. However, he had also criticized the massive U.S. military deployment and later would

strongly protest the heavy bombing of Iraq. Caught between severe Iraqi and Israeli pressures, he must have
known that such criticisms would be costly in his relations with the United States. He did indeed become
the target of political wrath that led to the suspension
of U.S. foreign aid to Jordan.

It wasn't until November 30, four months after the
invasion of Kuwait, that Bush proposed "discussions" (not "negotiations") between the United States
and Iraq in order to "go the extra mile for peace." He
suggested that he would receive Iraq's Foreign Minister, Tariq Aziz, in Washington, and also send Secretary Baker to see Saddam Hussein in Baghdad "at a
mutually convenient time between December 15th
and January 15th of next year." Coming as it did
when administration policy had been repeatedly challenged in Senate hearings and had suffered a severe
loss of public approval (which it had sought to recoup
by sounding alarms about Iraq's impending nuclear
threat), this promise of going "the extra mile for
peace" was another timely bid for domestic political
support. The proposal was immediately praised by
congressional leaders of both parties, by the press,
and by U.N. Secretary-General Javier Pérez de Cuéllar. Bob Woodward described the scene in the White
House's Cabinet Room later on November 30, when
the administration's "principals" were joined by the
congressional leadership:

> The announcement of the Baker mission had nearly all
> the two dozen men in a jocular, even boisterous mood.
> The atmosphere was like a men's clubhouse, with
> much back-slapping and joking. It only calmed down
> when Bush took his seat.[4]

Bush's "peace proposal" was clearly a popular move
and raised fresh hopes that war could be avoided.
Whether it would lead to a diplomatic success was another matter. After all, it had come just twenty-four

hours after the United States had pushed its "all necessary means" resolution through the U.N. Security
Council. Saddam Hussein, confronted with the threat
of force on November 29 and a "peace" initiative on
November 30, pointedly insisted on the word "negotiations" (instead of Bush's proposed "discussions") in
accepting Bush's suggestion. Throughout December,
Washington and Baghdad carried on an angry dispute
as to when and where talks might actually take place.

It was on December 6, in that Advent season when
the hopes and fears of the world were focused on the
prospects of peace talks, that the most constructive
and comprehensive design for approaching those
talks was offered to the Senate Foreign Relations
Committee. That design came from the person regarded by many as this nation's foremost scholar and
counselor on the arts of creative diplomacy, Professor
Roger Fisher of Harvard Law School, longtime director of the Harvard Negotiation Project and a veteran
of many efforts at peaceful settlement in various Middle East disputes.

The authors of this book regard Professor Fisher's
Senate testimony as having offered the most promising diplomatic approach to the prevention of a U.S.-
Iraq war, and also the explanation as to why U.S.
diplomacy never offered a realistic prospect of success. (Similar approaches were reportedly advocated
by Middle East specialists in the bowels of the bureau-
cracy at the State Department, but were never seriously entertained by the White House.)

Titled "How to Negotiate with Iraq Without Giving In," Fisher's testimony insisted that threats and
coercion were not enough. They had to be balanced
by incentives that would take account of Iraq's legitimate concerns and allow Saddam Hussein at least a
chance at the face-saving possibility of claiming success. Such incentives were described as "essential to
any peaceful outcome." But U.S. policy thus far had

only been "asking Saddam Hussein to jump out of the frying pan into the fire": withdrawal from Kuwait might still be followed by an attack on Iraq, an Iraqi loss of military prowess, Iraqi forfeiture of all disputes with Kuwait, war crime trials, and even Saddam's own downfall. Fisher said:

> Increasing the size of the threat to Hussein does not, by itself, provide a greater incentive for withdrawal. If sanctions and the threat of war are to have any chance of influencing Iraq to get out of Kuwait, Iraq needs to be confident that if it does get out sanctions and the threat of war will stop. Without rewarding aggression, it should be possible to convince Iraq that getting out of Kuwait is better than staying in.

Among Iraq's "possible legitimate concerns," Fisher listed Kuwait's pumping of oil from the disputed Rumaila oil field, Iraq's access to the Gulf for a deepwater port, fairer distribution of Arab wealth, the Palestinian cause, the double standard imposed in Iraq's being forced to comply with U.N. resolutions and to renounce chemical and nuclear weapons, and that a fair process for negotiating issues with Kuwait be established.

Fisher charged that Bush and his aides really had not been practicing diplomacy at all—at least not as the art of peacemaking:

> There has been much talk by the Administration that the purpose of the meeting [proposed by Bush November 30] is simply to communicate clearly to Saddam Hussein that if he wants to avoid war, he has no recourse but to withdraw—to make sure he "gets the message." Our purpose ought not to be narrow, one-way communication. President Bush and Secretary Baker ought not view their role as simply delivering an ultimatum; they should also be prepared to listen and to explore options for building a framework for a peaceful solution.

Fisher himself proposed such a framework in which the United States and Iraq might at least agree on the topics to be discussed. (Fisher suggested twelve such topics.) He outlined roles for the U.N. Secretary-General, U.N. peacekeeping and observer forces, and the Arab League.

Throughout that contentious December, it became increasingly clear that Tariq Aziz would never get to Washington, nor would Baker get to Baghdad. Finally, on January 9, six days before the U.N. deadline, Baker and Tariq Aziz met in Geneva. The six-hour meeting was a diplomatic failure. It had been preceded by a tough White House press statement promising that there would be "no negotiation, no compromises, no face-saving measures." In short, by Roger Fisher's conception, there would be no real diplomacy in Geneva. The Geneva meeting would offer a bizarre contradiction: diplomacy without negotiation. At meeting's end, Baker reported that he had made a serious "effort to find a political solution to the crisis in the Gulf. I met with Minister Aziz today not to negotiate, as we had made clear we would not do, . . . but I met with him today to communicate."

The main moment of drama in Geneva came when Foreign Minister Aziz revealed that he "declined to receive the letter from President Bush to my president" because, he said, the language of the letter was personally disrespectful and "full of threats." The text of Bush's letter read, in part:

> We prefer a peaceful outcome. . . . There can be no re-ward for aggression. Nor will there be any negotiation. Principle cannot be compromised. . . . But unless you withdraw from Kuwait completely and without condi-tion, you will lose more than Kuwait.

Immediately after the Geneva meeting, Bush held a White House press conference in which he referred to Aziz's refusal to receive his letter:

This is but one more example that the Iraqi government is not interested in direct communications, designed to settle the Persian Gulf situation. . . . The
conclusion is clear: Saddam Hussein continues to reject a diplomatic solution. I sent Secretary Jim Baker
to Geneva, not to negotiate, but to communicate. . . .
Let me emphasize that I have not given up on a peaceful outcome. It's not too late.

But of course it was too late. Diplomacy-as-
communication-of-threats-and-ultimatums—but "no
negotiation, no compromises, no face-saving measures"—had failed to prevent the war. Whether it had
been intended to do so is not yet clear. Had George
Bush really gone "the last mile for peace," as he promised and then claimed?

Other Diplomatic Efforts

No region in the world is vested with the interests
and emotions of more nations than the Middle East.
It is hardly surprising, therefore, that many individu-
als, governments, and multilateral institutions sought
to make peace in the Gulf after August 2.

Jimmy Carter's preference for the Arab states to assume regional responsibility for overcoming the Gulf
crisis was a reflection of the preference of most Arab
leaders themselves, at least initially. In fact, Article 52
of the United Nations Charter requires "every effort
to achieve pacific settlement of local disputes"
through regional agencies "before referring them to
the Security Council." Meeting in Cairo on August 3,
the Arab League Council's first response to Iraq's attack on Kuwait was to condemn the attack and call
for Iraq to withdraw. But the Council, with virtual
unanimity, declined Kuwait's request for immediate
application of the League's defense pact, which would
have meant collective military action. The Council

deferred to diplomatic efforts by King Hussein, who had promoted an "Arab solution" on a rapid circuit of Arab and European capitals and who called for an Arab summit, to which Saddam Hussein provisionally agreed. The king's own proposal envisioned an Iraqi withdrawal from Kuwait in return for possible concessions to Iraq, the convening of an international conference that would also address the conflicts on the West Bank and in Lebanon, and the deployment of U.N. or Arab forces rather than Western troops in Saudi Arabia. King Hussein was optimistic—so much so that when President Bush called him in the first hours after the Iraqi attack, Hussein replied: "We can solve this, George. Give me a bit of time."[5]

The Bush administration, however, had decided from the outset to prevent any "Arab solution," King Hussein's or any other. Reportedly scolding Arab governments for failing to take immediate military action against Iraq, the White House forthwith launched plans not only for U.S. military intervention but also for the overthrow of Saddam Hussein. According to Woodward, on August 3, while the Arab League was attempting a regional settlement, Bush directed the CIA "to begin planning for a covert operation that would destabilize the regime and, [Bush] hoped, remove Saddam from power." What the president wanted was "an all-fronts effort to strangle the Iraqi economy, support anti-Saddam resistance groups inside or outside Iraq, and look for alternative leaders in the military or anywhere in Iraqi society. . . . If ever there was a case for covert action undertaken in the national interest, he said, this was it."[6] Two days later, Secretary of Defense Cheney and General Schwarzkopf were off to Saudi Arabia to seek King Fahd's approval of the immediate deployment of U.S. forces. In three more days, Bush announced that deployment.

The next day, August 9, public responses throughout the Arab world to Bush's announcement took the form of large pro-Iraqi demonstrations in Jordan, Algeria, Tunisia, Mauritania, Sudan, Somalia, Yemen, and the occupied West Bank and Gaza Strip. Meanwhile, hundreds of thousands of Arab, Asian, and European nationals were fleeing Kuwait and Iraq, many of them trapped in the deserts of Jordan and Iraq. King Hussein continued his ricochet diplomacy, flying to Baghdad and then to Washington and Kennebunkport. In fruitless talks with Bush, he assured the president that his country, although opposed to Iraq's occupation of Kuwait and heavily burdened with the economic costs of the sanctions and blockade, would "not cease efforts at seeking an 'Arab' diplomatic solution." But Bush and his aides feared that Hussein's diplomatic efforts would undercut their military plans as well as U.N. sanctions. The king continued to believe that an "Arab solution" might well have induced Iraq to withdraw from Kuwait and prevented an all-out war, "but for U.S. intransigence and haste to send troops to the gulf."[7]

At an Arab summit conference in Cairo on August 10, twenty chiefs of state (minus Saddam Hussein, who sent his vice-premier) met to consider a variety of proposals for action. Resolutions adopted, at strong U.S. urging, supported Kuwait's sovereignty and independence, Saudi Arabia's legitimate self-defense, and the first U.N. resolutions. But these actions were far from unanimous. Iraq, Libya, and the PLO voted no. Algeria and Yemen abstained. Jordan, Sudan, and Mauritania expressed "reservations." Tunisia absented itself. Moreover, in a closed plenary session, Egypt's President Mubarak criticized Saudi Arabia for its precipitate acceptance of U.S. troops. The absent Saddam Hussein broadcast a message on Baghdad Radio calling for a *jihad* to save "Mecca and the tomb of the Prophet from occupation" by American forces. (Egypt, Morocco, Syria, and the smaller

Gulf states did eventually constitute, along with Saudi and Kuwaiti troops, a Pan-Arab Force as part of the Coalition against Iraq.)[8] Egypt's participation in the Coalition was solidified by the forgiveness of billions of dollars in debt to the United States. Syria's participation was secured by U.S. license to President Hafez al-Assad to intervene in Lebanon and wrest control of Beirut from Maronite General Michel Aoun—and probably also by generous cash offerings from Saudi Arabia and Kuwait.[9]

Perhaps the last notable Arab effort to mediate the Gulf crisis and avert war was that of Algerian President Chadli Bendjedid. After conversations with French President François Mitterrand in Paris on December 22, Chadli proposed that a "concrete signal on the Palestinian question would be a decisive step," presumably as a face-saving tactic to facilitate Saddam Hussein's withdrawal from Kuwait. In fact, Chadli consulted Saddam and reported that Iraq was prepared to pay "a certain price" to withdraw. (Four months earlier, in Baghdad on August 26, Saddam had told the PLO's Yasir Arafat that it would be politically easier for Iraq to withdraw if Saddam could claim to have helped solve "something like the Palestinian problem" than if he pulled out "only for the islands and the oil-fields.") Chadli's gambit, like King Hussein's, was rejected by Bush—and also by King Fahd.[10]

President Mitterrand made repeated efforts, from September of 1990 to January of 1991, to provide a diplomatic alternative to the rigidity of the U.S. line. On September 24, he outlined a four-stage proposal, in which he said: "If Saddam Hussein will affirm his intention to withdraw his troops, and liberate hostages, everything becomes possible." In particular, it was Mitterrand's willingness to envisage "linkage" of the Gulf crisis with other Middle East conflicts that attracted Iraq and other Arab states, but was repudiated by Bush. Mitterrand then traveled to Saudi Arabia and the United Arab Emirates for talks with their leaders, after which he continued to advocate an international conference that would deal with the Palestinian issue.

Several other European governments, responding to public sentiment, sought to make the European Community the instrument of peacemaking in the Gulf. Italy, Spain, Portugal, and Ireland were foremost among such advocates of a diplomatic alternative to U.S. policy. Italian Foreign Minister Gianni De Michelis, as chairman of the E.C. Council of Ministers, made two efforts in December to promote negotiations between the United States and Iraq. Both efforts were rebuffed by the Bush administration. A majority of European governments, in the face of "strong U.S. remonstrances," were finally convinced that "it was impossible for the E.C. to substitute itself for the U.S. in dealings with Iraq."[11]

At a meeting of European Community Foreign Ministers on January 4, France proposed a seven-point plan for peace talks, supported by Germany, that was conspicuously more flexible than the U.S. approach to the upcoming Geneva encounter on January 9 between James Baker and Tariq Aziz ("no negotiation, no compromises, no face-saving measures"). On January 10, a Mitterrand aide spoke hopefully of what a more general settlement of outstanding Middle East issues could yet accomplish. That French approach was urged, once more, on January 16, just hours before U.S. planes began the bombing of Baghdad. The unyielding opposition of the Bush administration (and of Israel) to any Arab or European approach that provided even face-saving "linkage" with Palestine perhaps doomed any diplomatic possibility of avoiding the war.

On deadline day, January 15, Pope John Paul II addressed urgent letters to both Bush and Saddam Hussein. To Bush, he wrote: "We cannot pretend that the use of arms, and especially of today's highly sophisticated weaponry, would not give rise, in addition to suffering and destruction, to new and perhaps worse injustices. . . . In these last hours . . . I truly hope, and I appeal with lively faith to the Lord, that peace can still be saved." To Saddam, he requested "a demonstration of readiness on your part" that "cannot fail to bring you honor before your beloved country, the region and the whole world. In these dramatic hours, I pray that God will enlighten you and grant you the strength to make a generous gesture which will avoid war."

Neither the Episcopalian nor the Muslim addressee, both of whom would soon escalate their respective religious rhetoric, yielded to the Roman Pontiff. On January 20, four days into the air war, Saddam promised that "the unjust will die and the 'God is Great' banner will flutter with great victory in the mother of all battles." Eight days later Bush assured the National Religious Broadcasters that "we know that, God willing, this is a war we will win."

Could United Nations Secretary-General Javier Pérez de Cuéllar have played a more positive role in attempting to negotiate an avoidance of war? Pérez de Cuéllar, perhaps the most resourceful diplomat to have held that post since the days of Dag Hammarskjöld three decades ago, no more anticipated the Iraqi invasion of Kuwait than did Arab leaders or Western intelligence; he was on vacation at the time of the attack. From the very first Security Council resolution of August 2, however, he was obliged to be the servant of the Council and the succession of resolutions that rationalized U.S. and Coalition actions against Iraq. He was caught in a crossfire between those who charged that he was not exercising his "good offices" independently and vigorously enough and those who charged that he was insufficiently subservient to U.S. interests. The Secretary-General was apparently never asked by the United States or the Security Council to assume the diplomatic initiative in mediating the conflict. What is less evident is the extent to which he was pressured by U.S. policy makers to refrain from serious mediation efforts that could complicate the drive toward an offensive military policy.

Having made an earlier trip to Amman to meet with Iraqi Foreign Minister Tariq Aziz, Pérez de Cuéllar flew to Baghdad on January 12, the day Congress was concluding its debate on presidential authority to initiate offensive military action. Bush, perhaps betraying some uncertainty as to how the Secretary-General would behave in Baghdad, said it might be acceptable to talk about some kind of peace conference, but "it depends on how it's put forward"— which led Elizabeth Drew to observe that "we might go to war over semantics."[12] The next day, Pérez de Cuéllar met with Saddam Hussein for over three hours; it was only four days since the Baker-Aziz meeting in Geneva. On January 14, in a confidential report to the Security Council, the Secretary-General said he had offered Saddam assurances that if Iraq withdrew from Kuwait, Iraq would not be attacked. But at that late hour, he still was not authorized to offer any positive incentives of a face-saving kind. As in Geneva, so in Baghdad: Saddam would not yield to the U.S./U.N. demands. Finally, on January 15, U.N. deadline day, the Security Council authorized the Secretary-General to issue a last-minute nonbinding statement that (sort of) hinted at the possibility of face-saving, after all. Pérez de Cuéllar issued such a statement, with its requisite vagueness:

> I must sincerely appeal to President Saddam Hussein to turn the course of events away from catastrophe and toward a new era of justice and harmony based on the

principles of the United Nations Charter. I have every assurance once again from the highest levels of government that with the resolution of the present crisis, every effort will be made to address, in a comprehensive manner, the Arab-Israeli conflict, including the Palestinian question.

But that was really to offer no more than U.S. rhetoric had offered for weeks: yes, the Palestinian question would have to be faced, but only after Iraq capitulated to all U.N. resolutions. Saddam Hussein did not deign to reply. The bombing of Baghdad began.

While a clear picture of Pérez de Cuéllar's own views and actions has yet to emerge, there are possible clues. He pointedly distanced himself from media characterizations of Security Council Resolution 678 ("all necessary means" after January 15) as a "U.N. deadline." Rather, he sought to interpret the time between November 29 and January 15 as a cooling-off period. He would not explicitly claim that Resolution 678 was a mandate for war.

Another possible clue (assuming it is not a fabrication or misrepresentation) is contained in an Iraqi transcript of the discussions between Pérez de Cuéllar and Saddam Hussein on January 13. Saddam is reported as charging that the Secretary-General was presenting *American,* not U.N. demands. The U.N. resolutions "are American resolutions. This is an American age. What America wants today is what happens." Pérez de Cuéllar is said to have replied: "I agree with you as far as the issue concerns me." He went on to commend Saddam for pressing the Palestinian issue and insuring its place on the U.N. agenda; he also said that agenda must include the removal of weapons of mass destruction (including Israel's) from the Middle East. The United Nations, on grounds of confidentiality, would neither confirm nor deny the accuracy of the Iraqi transcript.[13]

Three months later, in an address on April 16 to the European Parliament in Strasbourg, Secretary-General Pérez de Cuéllar made some rather remarkable comments:

> The victory of the allied, or coalition, countries over Iraq is not at all a victory for the United Nations, because this war was not its war. It was not a United Nations war. General Schwarzkopf was not wearing a blue helmet.

That disavowal was a direct contradiction of George Bush's March 6 victory speech to a joint session of Congress, in which the president claimed: "This is a victory for every country in the coalition and for the United Nations . . . a victory for the rule of law and for what is right."

Pérez de Cuéllar proceeded in the Strasbourg address to distinguish between a war legitimized by the Security Council and one actually directed and controlled by the United Nations. "The establishment of a new world order about which so much has been said will have to take place within the framework of the United Nations, but of a United Nations which does not resort to the use of double standards—a United Nations whose impartiality ensures its credibility."[14] That was a speech implicit with revelations yet to come about the Secretary-General's role in the Gulf crisis.

Gorbachev's Last Gambit

By January 16, 1991, all diplomatic efforts having failed both to persuade Saddam Hussein to withdraw from Kuwait and to dissuade George Bush from launching an air war, one other diplomatic question hovered over the Gulf and would remain there for the next five weeks: Could some fresh gambit negotiate the end of hostilities before the air war was joined by a ground war? A ground war would, predictably, involve the invasion of both Iraq and Kuwait; the multiplication of casualties; the further devastation of cities and the environment; the political problems of occupation, however temporary; and perhaps Iraq's use of chemical weapons.

It was to avoid such an expansion of the war (and no doubt to recoup some lost superpower status in the Middle East) that Mikhail Gorbachev undertook an independent peace initiative in February. In the first weeks after the invasion of Kuwait, Gorbachev had opposed any resort to military force, while supporting the condemnation of the invasion and the imposition of sanctions. In early October, he had dispatched his personal adviser, Yevgeni Primakov, on a well-publicized mission to Amman and Baghdad in quest of a "political solution" that would restore the *status quo ante bellum.* Primakov succeeded in arranging the withdrawal of the five thousand Soviet technicians and other citizens still in Iraq. But he also let it be known that he had talked with both Saddam Hussein and King Hussein about Iraqi withdrawal from Kuwait in return for concessions such as control of the contested Rumaila oil field and the islands that would secure a deep-water seaport. This was not welcome news to the Bush administration, intent as it was on humiliating Saddam and avoiding any compromises.

From the start, Gorbachev had maintained a certain distance from U.S. policy in the Gulf, while not obstructing it in the Security Council. In February, he made his last bid to mediate a peace settlement between Iraq and the Coalition. Primakov returned to Baghdad on February 12 for a meeting with Saddam Hussein, to whom he reported, "The Americans are determined to launch a large-scale ground operation to crush Iraqi forces in Kuwait." He delivered to Saddam Gorbachev's proposal that Saddam simply

announce the withdrawal of troops from Kuwait,
without conditions. Three days later, Iraq announced
its willingness to withdraw, in compliance with Security Council Resolution 660—on a number of conditions. Tariq Aziz shuttled back and forth between
Moscow and Baghdad as discussion of the conditions
and timing of troop pullout continued with Gorbachev very much personally engaged.

At 3:30 A.M. on February 22, Gorbachev's press
spokesman Vitali Ignatenko held a briefing to announce progress toward reaching an agreement on six
points, with discussion to continue. However, in a
ninety minute phone conversation with Gorbachev,
Bush indicated that he was dissatisfied with the So-
viet-Iraq talks. Bush doubted they would prove useful. He wanted a more rapid troop pullout than the
twenty-one days proposed. He wanted more satisfaction concerning POWs and the damage done to
Kuwait.

Only a few hours later, Bush pronounced his ultimatum: Iraq must begin its withdrawal by noon
(Washington time) the very next day, Saturday, February 23; must complete it within one week; and must
withdraw all forces from Kuwait City within the first
forty-eight hours. Saddam's failure to meet these
terms would mean the unleashing of a ground war.

At 2:00 A.M. Saturday (Moscow time; 6:00 P.M. Fri-
day Washington time), Gorbachev received a positive
reply from Saddam, followed by Tariq Aziz's announcement, in Moscow, that Iraq had agreed to "the
immediate and unconditional withdrawal of all its
armed forces from Kuwait." However, Aziz's statement was not entirely unconditional after all, because
it challenged the validity of Security Council actions
adopted after the initial Resolution 660 (assuming
Iraq's compliance with the resolution).

With eight hours remaining before Bush's deadline,
Gorbachev phoned Bush and other Coalition leaders

to urge a meeting of the Security Council in view of the "new situation" created by the Iraqi decision to withdraw. In the March 11 issue of *Time* magazine, Yevgeni Primakov concluded his inside account of the last hours before the ground war began with this lamentation:

> In Gorbachev's view the differences between the formula to which Iraq had agreed and the proposals from a number of other countries were not so great that they could not be worked out in the Security Council in one or two days. Certainly these differences were not so substantial that they justified a further escalation of the war. The Soviet U.N. representative was instructed to request an emergency session of the Security Council. However, as dawn broke on Feb. 24, the ground offensive of the multinational coalition began.[15]

As it was with all the others who had attempted to use negotiations to end the Gulf crisis, so it was with Mikhail Gorbachev: George Bush would have none of it. Bush had preceded his disclosure of the details of his ultimatum to Saddam with a faint reference to "the Soviet initiative, which very frankly we appreciate"—but followed it with uncompromising terms and a timetable that would make it impossible for Gorbachev to succeed.

6

Legitimate Authority?
War Powers
in Desert Storm

Armed with the political cohesion of the anti-Iraq Coalition, the parade of U.N. resolutions, and the approval of Congress, the Bush administration clearly succeeded in establishing the legitimacy of its resort to war in the Gulf—at least, established it to the satisfaction of most of the world's major governments, and of American politicians and legal scholars. Although there was some debate about the issue of authority before January 12, 1991 (the day Congress ratified the Security Council resolutions), such debate as there was after January 12 tended to focus on other issues.

Fred Strasser, Washington bureau chief of *The National Law Journal,* observed several weeks after the ceasefire that

> This war was started, fought, and is being followed with more attention to law—international law—than any conflict in history. . . . From the start, events in the Gulf progressed with incredible, legalistic order. The objectives of the war were established by legal action of the Security Council under the United Nations' "constitution," its Charter. Likewise, Iraq's defeat was

acknowledged not at a meeting of generals in the desert, but on a piece of paper handed to the UN Secretary General in New York. During the war, our military leaders talked often and clearly about the Geneva Conventions, and how scrupulously they were complying with the ban against aiming at civilian targets.

Strasser went on to note the casting of Saddam as an "outlaw" for his "illegal" invasion of Kuwait and his failure to comply with international law concerning prisoners of war and noncombatants; proposals for war crimes trials in the manner of the Nuremberg and Tokyo trials; and potential U.N. legal machinery to adjudicate damage claims against Iraq ("the biggest tort court the world has ever seen").[1]

Twelve resolutions passed by the U.N. Security Council between August 2 and November 29, 1990, provided the legal foundation for the Bush Administration's claims of legitimate authority. Three of these twelve were most important:

—*Resolution 660* (August 2), in which the Security Council condemned the invasion of Kuwait and demanded that "Iraq withdraw immediately and unconditionally all its forces."

—*Resolution 661* (August 6), which approved mandatory economic sanctions under Article VII of the U.N. Charter, thus imposing a trade and financial embargo on Iraq.

—*Resolution 678* (November 29), which set a deadline of January 15, 1991, for Iraq to comply with Resolution 660 "and all subsequent relevant resolutions," and which "authorize[d] Member States co-operating with the Government of Kuwait . . . to use all necessary means to uphold and implement" those resolutions, should Iraq fail to comply by January 15.

Four of the remaining nine resolutions (665, 666, 669, and 670) implemented provisions of 660 concerning sanctions.

Three resolutions (664, 667, and 674) concerned Iraq's treatment of foreign nationals, hostages, diplomats, and diplomatic and consular facilities. The other two resolutions (662 and 667) guaranteed the sovereignty of Kuwait against Iraq's claim of annexation and condemned Iraq's destruction of Kuwait's civil and demographic records.

The Bush administration's success in mobilizing support for these resolutions (with only Cuba and Yemen casting any negative votes) was marked by increasingly enthusiastic rhetoric about the conflict's offering a "defining moment for a new world order." On January 28, Bush told the National Religious Broadcasters that

> a just war must also be declared by legitimate authority. Operation Desert Storm is supported by unprecedented United Nations solidarity, the principle of collective self-defense, 12 Security Council resolutions and, in the Gulf, 28 nations from six continents united—resolute that we will not waiver and that Saddam's aggression will not stand.

Granting the possibility that Bush's new reliance on international law "stems from nothing but expediency," Fred Strasser believes that it

> may well signal a historic change in perception. . . . Now, the U.S. has set a new standard for itself as the enforcer of international law. . . . But now, having laid down the law and set an example for less powerful members of the international family, the U.S. may be forced to follow its own leadership.[2]

Similarly, Lawrence D. Weiler, veteran U.S. diplomat and arms control specialist, suggests that the Gulf

War has been marked by "some potentially positive precedents concerning the United Nations and respect for international law embodied in the U.N. Charter." Weiler particularly notes U.S. military restraint shown in its withholding both enforcement of a naval blockade and resort to action beyond a blockade until Security Council resolutions authorized such actions.

> Before the world, the U.S. has proclaimed a policy of resisting aggression and maintaining security through the structures of the United Nations. If genuinely adhered to as an example of international constitutional restraint against unilateral intervention, that can be a turning point in history. Reinforcing this precedent will not be an easy task.[3]

The Ambiguities of Authority

The issue of legitimacy stretches beyond the letter of the law to matters of ethics and politics, and ultimately to justice. The texts of the U.N. resolutions do not, by themselves, settle the question of legitimate authority in the Gulf crisis. Ambiguities remain.

Our review of the traditional requirement of *last resort* in the previous chapter leads to the most serious doubts as to whether the Bush administration complied with the U.N. Charter's obligations under Chapter VI's "Pacific Settlement of Disputes." Specifically, Article 33 requires "the parties to any dispute . . . first of all, [to] seek a solution by negotiation, enquiry, mediation, conciliation, arbitration, judicial settlement, resort to regional agencies or arrangements, or other peaceful means of their own choice." Bush's disdain for the very word "negotiation" and his determined rejection of an "Arab solution" or mediation by any other government or regional institution suggest that the Charter was, at best, only selectively and prejudicially invoked.

Similarly, with regard to economic sanctions, Article 42 requires a determination by the Security Council that sanctions "would be inadequate or have proved to be inadequate" before authorizing military action. However, the Security Council never made such a determination. In fact, the embargo and blockade authorized by the Council were generally believed to be the most effective sanctions ever imposed against any nation. The administration's own rhetoric claimed as much—but the procedural requirements of Article 42 were ignored.

Not yet as open to view are U.S. political pressures, inducements, and compromises to obtain favorable votes in the Security Council on Gulf crisis resolutions. Soviet and Chinese support were obviously critical in view of the veto possibility. Bush's rhetorical restraint in the face of harsh Soviet measures toward several independence-minded republics within the USSR, as well as assurances concerning aid and trade, may have been necessary (or been *felt* necessary) to secure Soviet votes. There were some semantic compromises in the drafting of the climactic Resolution 678. After Bush's November 8 doubling of U.S. forces as a move toward gaining an "offensive military option," the Soviet leadership continued to resist a U.N. license for the "use of force" and to refrain from committing troops to the Coalition. It was finally at the insistence of Foreign Minister Eduard Shevardnadze, in protracted discussion with Secretary Baker, that Resolution 678 euphemistically authorized "all necessary means" and made no mention of "force." Gorbachev personally insisted that the six weeks between November 29 and January 15 be designated within the resolution as "a pause of goodwill." It was done.[4]

China's implicit veto threat was perhaps a more serious obstacle to pro-U.S. votes. Chinese leaders had good reason to view the Gulf crisis as an opportunity to overcome their country's political isolation after the 1989 massacre in Tiananmen Square and subsequent repressions. Senator Tom Harkin (D-Iowa), by his January 3 refusal of unanimous consent to adjourn the Senate for three weeks without a vote on authorizing offensive action, helped guarantee the congressional debate and votes. Harkin took to the floor to question U.S. behavior at the United Nations. He noted that, after Congress had adjourned in October and after the November elections, not only had Bush doubled U.S. troops in the Gulf but also had obtained the January 15 deadline from the United Nations:

> Secretary Baker went around the world, getting all the nations to support the vote in the U.N. Security Council. This senator wonders, and I wonder aloud, what Secretary Baker promised all these nations to get them to vote for this resolution? I would note for the record that the day after the U.N. vote when China abstained—they could have vetoed the resolution, but China abstained—the day after, the Chinese foreign minister had a meeting with the president at the White House. After what happened in the Tiananmen Square last year, what did Secretary Baker promise China to get them to abstain in the Security Council? I think that is a question that needs to be answered.

Perhaps that question was answered by Bush's strong push for most favored nation (MFN) status for China after the Gulf War ended—over strong congressional opposition.

It may be years, if ever, before the full costs of those Security Council votes are known. Colombia, Ethiopia, Finland, the Ivory Coast, Malaysia, Romania, and Zaire were all members of the Council in 1990 who voted "yes" on all twelve resolutions; the record of their rewards is not yet available.

The heavy political role played by the United States

in forging U.N. policies during the Gulf crisis was matched by the operational unilateralism of the United States in decision-making, strategic planning, military command, and conduct of the war. As in the Korean War forty years earlier, the United Nations provided a kind of juridical and moral cover for the United States and its allies. But it was George Bush who decided whether and when to initiate both the air war and the ground war, while the world waited for his unilateral decisions. The Security Council played no role in organizing military operations. American generals did that. American bombers, missiles, ships, and troops were the decisive forces in the war. As Secretary-General Pérez de Cuéllar said after it was all over: "It was not a United Nations war. General Schwarzkopf was not wearing a blue helmet."

As the war's destructiveness mounted, reflecting the escalating intentions of George Bush, there was a growing sentiment in many countries—including Coalition allies and especially Arab nations that had joined in condemning Saddam Hussein's invasion—that the United Nations had been politically misused and morally degraded by the war. Such sentiment was reinforced by judgments that U.S. attacks on Iraq's civilian infrastructure and the slaughter of thousands of retreating troops far exceeded any U.N. mandate. Some members of Congress shared that judgment. In a speech to the National Press Club on January 24, barely a week after the beginning of the air war, Representative Lee Hamilton (D-Ind.), chairman of the House Middle East Subcommittee, declared that Bush's

> recent statements and our military actions suggest that our goals are expanding to include the surrender of Iraq and the destruction of its military. These objectives stretch the meaning of the 12 United Nations resolutions. . . . Sometimes, I think we Americans be-

lieve that war solves all our problems. It may solve some, but it will create and worsen others. In the end, most of the objectives we have sought militarily will also have to be negotiated.

At war's end, Hamilton wrote:

We have not recognized the war's true costs. How do you calculate the cost of not only coalition casualties . . . but an estimated 80,000 to 100,000 Iraq casualties? How do you estimate the cost of reconstructing devastated cities? How do you measure the cost of the environmental damage to the air and waters of the Persian Gulf and the cost of destroyed oil wells and facilities?[5]

At Strasbourg in April, Secretary-General Pérez de Cuéllar pleaded for "a United Nations which does not resort to the use of double standards—a United Nations whose impartiality ensures its credibility." He was clearly sensitive to the charge that the United Nations (or the nations dominating the U.N.) had indeed practiced double standards in dealing with the world's conflicts, a fact blatantly exposed by the U.N.'s response to the Gulf crisis and also tending to diminish the U.N.'s moral authority.

The National Council of Churches had raised this concern much earlier, in its November 15, 1990, "Resolution on the Gulf and Middle East Crisis." U.S. and U.N. actions against Iraq stood "in marked contrast to U.S. negligence regarding the implementation of Security Council resolutions 242 and 338" calling for withdrawal of Israeli troops from occupied territories and action on the Palestinian issue. Similar negligence was charged concerning implementation of Security Council resolutions 359, 360, and 361, which called for withdrawal of Turkish troops from Cyprus.[6]

In a scathing critique of U.S. "use (and abuse) of the United Nations," Noam Chomsky added to the list of double standards:

> The U.N. was able to respond to Iraq's aggression be-
> cause—for once—the U.S. happened to be opposed to
> criminal acts, as distinct from the invasions of Pan-
> ama, Cyprus, Lebanon, the Western Sahara, and much
> else. For decades, South Africa defied the U.N. and the
> World Court on Namibia, looting and terrorizing the
> occupied country and using it as a base for its terror
> and aggression against neighboring states. . . . No one
> proposed bombing South Africa. . . . The U.S. advo-
> cated "quiet diplomacy" and "constructive engage-
> ment" . . . .

Chomsky also mentioned a long string of U.S. vetoes
of Security Council resolutions, including those condemning the U.S. invasion of Panama (called "Operation Just Cause" by the Bush administration) and
Israeli abuses of Palestinian rights.[7]

Ultimately, hopes for Lawrence Weiler's "potentially positive precedents" for the United Nations and
for a genuinely new "new world order" depend on re-
versing the entire pattern of U.S. policy toward the
United Nations over the past dozen years. While the
USSR has become a more engaged and constructive
U.N. member, paying its dues promptly, the United
States had become the United Nations' number one
delinquent and dropout, and a downright obstruc-
tionist in most fields of international cooperation.
U.S. nonpayment of assessments to the regular U.N.
budget, peacekeeping operations, and special agencies
rose to over $700 million, or 70 percent of the United
Nations' total arrearages. (At last, in November 1990,
as the United States was seeking U.N. support for its
planned war in the Gulf, President Bush signed legislation providing for full payment of dues and a 20
percent downpayment on back dues.) Reagan-Bush
rejection of World Court jurisdiction in the case of
U.S. warfare against Nicaragua; repudiation of the
Law of the Sea Treaty; refusal of any minimal U.N.

norms in world trade, aid, money, and debt; withdrawal from several specialized agencies; withholding
of money from the U.N. Population Fund because of
its support of family planning programs; and obstruction of a U.N. consensus on a comprehensive nuclear
test ban—these are among the many aspects of an
anti-U.N. posture that has severely impaired prospects for an authoritative new world order.

In the Carnegie Endowment study, *Estrangement:
America and the World,* Richard Ullman observes that
"the most significant estrangement" of the United
States in recent years has been "from the entire idea of
cooperation through a formal structure of international organization," especially the United Nations—
an estrangement that has "verged on contempt" for
the rest of the world.[8] Beyond the hard-lobbied-for
U.N. seal for U.S. military policies in the Gulf, the
Bush administration (like the Reagan administration)
has shown little disposition to strengthen the political
and moral authority of the United Nations on the great
constructive tasks of world order, human development, and global survival.

Congressional Approval

After obtaining Resolution 678 from the U.N. Security Council, George Bush and his aides repeatedly
claimed that the president had adequate authority to
initiate offensive warfare without any congressional
action. Meeting with congressional leaders November
30, Bush said: "If the Congress wants to come back
and endorse the U.N. resolution, let's go. But let's not
have a hung jury. If you can't support, frankly, I'd be
wary." Both Speaker Tom Foley and Senate Majority
Leader George Mitchell, however, were emphatic in
insisting that a congressional vote was necessary and
constitutionally required.[9] Article I, Section 8 of the
U.S. Constitution says, "The Congress shall have

power . . . to declare war . . . [and] to raise and support armies . . . [and] to provide and maintain a navy."

When Foley and Mitchell announced on January 7 that both houses of Congress would debate that week a resolution authorizing the use of force against Iraq, Bush immediately drafted a letter to Congress requesting endorsement of the "all necessary means" wording of Security Council Resolution 678. The President's lawyers continued to insist that he had adequate authority as commander-in-chief to conduct military operations. Deputy Attorney General William P. Barr told Bush that presidents had ordered military action more than two hundred times, but there had been only five declarations of war—none since 1941.[10] Warfare in Korea, Vietnam, the Dominican Republic, Grenada, Libya, and Panama had been waged without a congressional declaration of war under Article I, Section 8. Nevertheless, most of his legal and political aides advised Bush that his political authority would be greatly enhanced by congressional endorsement.

Congress, having adjourned in October for the midterm elections and having resisted any definitive action on the use of force, returned in January just a few days before the United Nations' deadline of January 15. Whatever the political calculations of the White House, Congress was confronted with a Hobson's choice: to reject Bush's request would be to reject the authority of the United Nations Security Council. On the other hand, a vote to endorse Resolution 678 would give the president a blank check as to whether or when to wage war against Iraq. With congressional voting set for Saturday, January 12, there was an additional pressure on the legislators. That very day, Secretary-General Pérez de Cuéllar was off to Baghdad for one last effort to persuade Saddam Hussein to comply with the U.N. resolutions. To fail to back the

United Nations' authority at that moment was all but unthinkable.

Nevertheless, both houses of Congress did debate and did vote. In opening the Senate debate, Senator George Mitchell said: "Today the Senate undertakes a solemn constitutional responsibility, to decide whether to commit the nation to war." Mitchell challenged Bush on the November 8 decision to double the troops in the Gulf in order to attain a "credible offensive option." Not only the decision itself but the way it was made particularly troubled the senator:

> The president did not consult with Congress about that decision. He did not try to build support for it among the American people. He just did it. . . . In effect, the president overnight, with no consultation and no public debate, changed American policy from being part of a collective effort to enforce economic and political sanctions into a predominantly American effort relying upon the use of American military force. As a result, this country has been placed on a course toward war.

Contrariwise, Senator Arlen Specter (R-Pa.) offered his judgment that "if the Congress of the United States does not back the president, and the Congress of the United States does not back Resolution 678, then our leadership will fail completely, the sanctions will disintegrate, and the coalition will disintegrate."

Senator Daniel Patrick Moynihan (D-N.Y.) warned against the dangers of a "Doctor Strangelove" war against Iraq, adding: "There seem to be people who are saying, 'Oh my God, we missed World War III' [a reference to the end of the Cold War]. 'Maybe we can have it here.' " Speaking in support of a prosanctions resolution he cosponsored with Mitchell, Senator Sam Nunn (D-Ga.), who certainly carried a number of votes against the president, declared:

Iraq is isolated and suffering from the embargo, and time is on our side. . . . In short, we are playing a winning hand. I see no compelling reason to rush to military action.

In support of Bush, Republican Leader Bob Dole (Kansas) chided the Democratic leadership for not acting earlier and asserted that Congress should not try to intervene "now, at the eleventh hour, having been AWOL for three or four months, and try to change the direction of the policy that President Bush has so patiently and successfully put together."

A chief sponsor of the pro-Bush resolution on the House side, Minority Leader Bob Michel (R-Ill.) seemed particularly impatient for the war to begin:

I understand principled pacifism. . . . What I cannot understand is a policy that asks us to believe that after six months or a year:
—The alliance will still hold.
—Our sophisticated equipment will be in better shape than it is now after frying in the desert.
—Our troops will have higher morale and better readiness.

In a rare floor speech, Speaker Foley closed the debate with "a public prayer for this House, for all of us, for the Congress, for our president—and he is our president—and for the American people, in particular those young Americans who stand ready to make the supreme sacrifice."

Then came the votes on that Saturday, January 12. The Senate voted 52 to 47, the House 250 to 183, to support Bush, Security Council Resolution 678, and the January 15 deadline. Those votes came after similar tallies rejected the Mitchell-Nunn resolution to continue Bush's earlier strategy of reliance on economic sanctions and diplomatic pressure.

After the votes—even more, after the air war began

just four days later—most senators and representatives felt they should close ranks, stop the debate, and
support the troops. To a large extent, the media and
the clergy followed suit. George Bush was in command. He had his war.

Two poignant questions remain.

Bush and his aides had continually urged support of
Security Council Resolution 678 as a strategy for
peace that would persuade Saddam Hussein to pull
out of Kuwait (although in the last hours just before
the votes the administration signaled to some key
members that these were probably votes for war). Just
after the congressional votes, the president held a
news conference in which he continued to claim that
his authority to wage war was the "best chance for
peace." How many senators—and there were at least
a few—honestly believed they were voting for peace
and not for war in supporting Bush is a haunting question, in view of the narrow margin in the Senate: three
more votes could have defeated Bush.

The other question is also of the "what-if" variety:
What if sanctions had been allowed to continue without the resort to war? What if they had been reinforced by more earnest and imaginative diplomatic
efforts? Congressman Lee Hamilton, understandably
sensitive to the possibility that those who voted
against Bush on January 12 would be called "wrong"
and "appeasers" (especially after the quick and overwhelming military victory), took to the Op-Ed page of
The Washington Post to ask, "Who Voted 'Wrong'?"

> First, it is flawed logic to assert that if one strategy
> proved successful, the other strategy was wrong. The
> success of the president's war strategy does not prove
> that his original strategy of economic sanctions, diplo-
> matic pressure and a credible military option would
> have failed. . . . But when we chose the war option, we
> foreclosed a chance to find out whether the president's

original strategy would have worked. . . . Many members of Congress were uncomfortable giving the president that total authority to wage war. They believed that the Constitution requires shared responsibility at the time a decision to go to war is made. . . . Were we wrong . . . ?[11]

Congressman Hamilton credits the president's strategy with success—which is to raise the next criterion of the just war tradition: a reasonable *prospect of success.* And just what is "success" in the Middle East now, after the "victory" in the Gulf War?

7

Prospect of Success?
Expectations of Victory

The dominant mood of the U.S. government as the Gulf War began was the anticipation of success, with only the timing and the cost unknown. And the dominant political reality in the nation at the end of the war was jubilation, even euphoria, in the wake of a swift and spectacular victory. The canons of success, however, would prove to be morally and politically problematical.

In his address to the nation on January 16, 1991, announcing the beginning of the Coalition air attack against Iraq, President Bush said:

> Now the 28 countries with forces in the Gulf area have exhausted all reasonable efforts to reach a peaceful solution—have no choice but to drive Saddam from Kuwait by force. We will not fail. . . . Prior to ordering our forces into battle, I instructed our military commanders to take every necessary step to prevail as quickly as possible, and with the greatest degree of protection possible for American and allied service men and women. I've told the American people before that this will not be another Vietnam, and I repeat this here tonight. Our troops will have the best possible support

in the entire world, and they will not be asked to fight with one hand tied behind their back.

Speaking to the Religious Broadcasters on January 28, Bush noted:

> [W]ar must never, ever be undertaken without total commitment to a successful outcome. It is only justified when victory can be achieved. I have pledged that this will not be another Vietnam. . . . We will prevail because of the support of the American people, armed with a trust in God and in the principles that make men [*sic*] free. . . . We know that this is a just war. And we know that, God willing, this is a war we will win.

Prospects for success in war can be measured in two ways: (1) Is the military force large enough, strong enough, prepared and equipped enough to defeat the other side's military force? and (2) is the resort to military force, in fact, likely to attain the intended goals? The former is a matter of largely quantifiable military assessment; the latter is a political judgment.

The Military Balance

By early January total Coalition forces were estimated at 615,000 to 660,000 troops. The United States had committed 430,000 troops, of whom 370,000 were considered combat-ready at war's beginning, to the cause. Five other nations—Saudi Arabia, Egypt, the United Kingdom, Syria, and France, as well as the Gulf Cooperation Council—had pledged 10,000 or more troops, although Egypt, Syria, and France all indicated that they had grave reservations about taking any offensive action.[1] U.S. forces were supported by about 2,000 tanks, 1,300 aircraft, and more than 100 ships, including six aircraft carriers. According to published estimates, Iraqi forces totaled about 555,000 regular troops and 480,000 reserves, of whom 540,000 were estimated to be in southern Iraq and occupied Kuwait and 120,000 along Iraq's northern border with Turkey. Iraq's forces were thought to be supported by some 4,000 tanks, 500 combat aircraft and a negligible navy.[2]

Of course, numbers do not constitute the entire military assessment. Well before the war began, the Center for Defense Information compared U.S. and Iraqi strengths. Iraqi forces would be battle-hardened, and would be defending their homeland, fighting on familiar terrain with weapons adjusted to a desert environment, threatening to resort to chemical weapons, and exploiting anti-American sentiment in other Arab states. U.S. forces would be equipped with better intelligence, mobility, logistical support, and vastly superior air weapons, and would be enjoying a larger manpower pool and the commitment of Allied forces.[3] In envisioning possible war scenarios, the Center for Defense Information predicted that U.S. military forces would ultimately prevail, as did most others inside and outside of government. But the CDI also predicted, as did most others, much higher Coalition casualties than turned out to be the case.

The quick success of the military campaign, when it did come, made the prospects for military success seem more self-evident with hindsight than they did before the fact. In his introduction to a July 16, 1991, Pentagon report on lessons learned from the war, Defense Secretary Cheney wrote, "This victory was neither easy nor certain, although in hindsight it may have come to seem both." U.S. casualty planning assumed a longer, bloodier war (for the Coalition) than actually occurred. After November 1990, Central Command wanted 18,100 hospital beds ready in the war area, a number not reached until mid-February. Many thousand more beds were made ready in hospitals and other military facilities in Europe and the United States. U.S. commanders guessed in November that the first twelve days of combat might yield 10,000 Allied dead.[4] The International Physicians for the Prevention of Nuclear War reported on January 11, 1991, that some 60,000 body bags had been or would be shipped to the Gulf.

While the case for military success was clouded with some uncertainties, U.S. political and military leaders clearly had a reasonable prospect of ultimately defeating the forces of Iraq.

The Political Goals

The case for a reasonable hope of success becomes more complicated when the criterion is whether a military campaign can and will achieve its political goals. As goals escalated in the months between August and January, it was impossible to maintain a consistent way to assess achievability. Would a military campaign protect Saudi Arabia from Iraqi invasion? Probably, but simply to place U.S. and Coalition forces in the northern Saudi desert was, demonstrably, to achieve that goal already without direct military action. Would a campaign succeed in getting Iraq out of Kuwait? Defeating the Iraqi army would indeed get it out. Yet twentieth-century warfare is full of examples of places destroyed in order to be "saved." It was not clear that, with the occupying Iraqi force dug in in an urban area, enough force could be used to compel Iraqi withdrawal without destroying Kuwait City as well.

Would a military campaign succeed in protecting Western oil interests in the region? Again, the answer is ambiguous. If the occupying force was driven out of Kuwait, control of Kuwaiti oil fields would also be wrested from Iraq. But the prospect of a war also presented the most likely scenario for physical destruction of oil fields and facilities, thus incapacitating Kuwaiti oil production. There was no reasonable hope that a war could prevent devastation of the oil fields and facilities.

Would a war eliminate Iraq as Israel's main rival and military threat in the region? Yes and no. If an air war could successfully find and destroy much of Iraq's military, including the missiles and chemical weapons holding special terrors for Israel, then the direct military threat to Israel would be reduced. If Iraq were able to hide or salvage much military hardware and personnel, then the threat would be increased. A war would likely increase Iraqi hatred for the "Western imperialists" and make Iraq even more vengefully disposed toward Israel as their perceived agent in the region. Defeat and humiliation ("success," from the U.S. perspective) would exacerbate Iraqi calls for later vengeance and vindication, thus increasing long-range instability and other problems for Israel in the region.

Would a war eliminate Iraq's chemical weapons capacity and nuclear weapons potential? Maybe—if the chemical weapons themselves, their production facilities, and the nuclear research facilities could be found and destroyed quickly enough. But if some were missed, then a war would dramatically increase incentive to actually use them. In the August 1991 *National Geographic,* eyewitness photographer Steve McCurry speculated that a howling desert wind- and sandstorm that occurred on the second and third days of the ground war was the main reason chemical weapons were not used on allied forces:

> The winds could also have been a lifesaver. Blowing directly toward Iraq's arsenal of chemical and nerve-gas rocket launchers, they may have rendered those weapons useless.[5]

The United Nations Security Council's cease-fire resolution requires Iraq to hand over to the United Nations for removal or destruction all weapons-grade nuclear material, chemical and biological weapons, and ballistic missiles. In the months after the cease-fire Iraq was notoriously evasive in complying with those provisions. Iraq cannot help but notice the difference between U.S. treatment of Iraq and of the Soviet Union. In forty years of Cold War with the Soviet Union (which possessed nuclear weapons), the United States never launched direct hostilities against it, while the United States turned to war against Iraq (which presumably did not yet possess nuclear weapons) after only five months of confrontation. Iraqis might understandably come to think that the way to prevent this humiliation from happening to them again would be to salvage as much of their nuclear weapons program as possible by circumventing U.N. oversight and then working faster than ever to get their own nuclear weapons.

Would a war succeed in eliminating Saddam Hussein himself? Probably not, if the war's primary aim was to drive Iraq from Kuwait and then stop. Maybe, if the war's aim was total defeat of the Iraqi army in Iraq and Saddam's unconditional surrender. The extraordinary fortifications of Saddam's own command bunker, built with German help, were public knowledge, and hunting expeditions for his "Wanderlodge" mobile command center bus proved fruitless. But while President Bush repeatedly urged Saddam's ouster, U.S. military strategy was never committed to that aim. In the early days after the cease-fire, the administration seemed to be counting on the possibility of a Sunni coup from within the Iraqi military. When, at Bush's urging, Kurds in the north and Shiites in the south rebelled against Saddam's regime in March, the United States refused them any military support, apparently preferring the relative stability of a weakened Saddam to the chaos that otherwise might split Iraq apart.

Would a war succeed in mobilizing public opinion

in the United States on behalf of the administration conducting it? Maybe, if the images of and information about the war could be adequately controlled. Americans do, after all, have a tendency to rally 'round in times of crisis. But if the war dragged on, if large numbers of American families began to lose loved ones, if the press got out of control, if Israel got sucked in, if chemical weapons were used, if the Coalition collapsed—then public opinion could easily turn away from supporting the war.

The moral and even religious confidence in military victory had its material basis in the incomparable destructive power of U.S. military forces. The fervent anticipation of triumph in a just war would, in a surprisingly short time, seem to be vindicated in the overwhelming successes of U.S. strategy and weaponry. And, indeed, the immediate and overwhelming sentiment of political and military leaders, the media, and most of the public—and this was evident from the televised spectacle of the high-tech bombing of Baghdad and the decimation of Iraq's retreating soldiers—would be a macho triumphalism already well-fed by the righteous conviction that America had just finished winning the Cold War. In his March 6 victory speech to a joint session of Congress, President Bush proclaimed:

> Tonight we meet in a world blessed by the promise of peace. From the moment Operation Desert Storm commenced on January 16 until the guns fell silent at midnight one week ago, this nation has watched its sons and daughters with pride—watched over them with prayer. . . . Our Armed Forces fought with honor and valor. . . . The America we saw in Desert Storm was first-class talent. And they did it using America's state-of-the-art technology. We saw the excellence embodied in the Patriot missile and the patriots who made it work. . . . There is something noble and ma-

jestic about the pride, about the patriotism, that we
feel tonight.

The relief and joy of service members' families wel-
coming them home from the Gulf were amplified by
the jubilant fervor of crowds and parades, and also by
the festive rhetoric of politicians—even those initially
opposed to the war, who were now positioning themselves to share in the aura of victory. Some returnees
found the hoopla disorientingly out of proportion to
their own few days' experience of war. Lewis H.
Lapham, editor of *Harper's,* explains:

> Americans tend to think of foreign affairs in terms of
> sporting events that allow for unambiguous results. Ei-
> ther the team wins or it loses; the game is over within a
> reasonable period of time, and everybody can go back
> to doing something else.[6]

President Bush called for National Days of Thanksgiving on April 5–7, "to give thanks to Almighty God
for liberation of Kuwait, for blessings of peace and
liberty, for our troops, our families, and our Nation."
In city after city throughout the land, the celebrations
and fireworks continued. And the parade of patriotic
holidays—Memorial Day, Flag Day, the Fourth of
July—that followed were coopted by the proud proc-
lamation that the "Vietnam syndrome" was overcome at last.

This fervor of presumed success began to fade during the summer of 1991. After all, Saddam Hussein
had not only survived the war but impudently dared
to claim a moral victory (in accepting a cease-fire, the
Iraqi government had not actually surrendered to a
multi-dozen coalition of greater and lesser powers).
Saddam righteously claimed to have raised the
world's consciousness of Palestinian grievances, the
poverty of most Arab peoples, the autocracy of oil-
rich sheikhdoms, the imperialism of Western oil in-

terests, and U.N. double standards concerning nuclear and chemical weapons. These are indeed significant moral issues that expose some of the failings of U.S. policies.

Of course, Saddam's personal claims to morality are fraudulent in the extreme. He has compounded the poverty of his own people, ruled as autocratically as any Arab leader, profited from Western imperialism, and deceived U.N. authorities for years. U.S. pride was further wounded by the fact that a large portion of Saddam's army and weaponry survived the Gulf War intact and then inflicted vast suffering on Iraq's own Shiite and Kurdish communities, terrorizing millions into abandoning their homes and becoming refugees in the most miserable of environments. Contrary to administration claims, Iraq's nuclear, chemical, and biological weapon capabilities had not all been destroyed. And when, after the cease-fire, a more candid account of U.S. military conduct was disclosed, many wondered whether the war that had seemed such a glittering military success was actually a dismaying moral and political failure. The very canons of success were proving to be misconceived.

8

Discrimination?
Scrupulous Conduct in War

We turn now to the *jus in bello* part of the just war ethic, the moral claims that apply during the actual conduct of a war.

Perhaps no single principle of the just war tradition received a more fulsome invocation by U.S. political and military leaders during the Gulf War than the principle of *discrimination:* avoiding harm to civilians, and renouncing massacres and wanton violence. The persistent repetition of moral claims about strictly limited targets, combined with televisible demonstrations of precision-guided bombs and missiles, persuaded much of the public that U.S. conduct in this war had achieved unprecedented heights of ethical sensitivity.

In his January 16 address announcing the beginning of the air war, President Bush assured the world: "We have no argument with the people of Iraq. Indeed, for the innocents caught in this conflict, I pray for their safety." Twelve days later he told the Religious Broadcasters:

> From the very first day of the war, the allies have waged war against Saddam's military. We are doing

everything possible, believe me, to avoid hurting the innocent. Saddam's response? Wanton, barbaric bombing of civilian areas. America and her allies value life. We pray that Saddam Hussein will see reason. To date, his indiscriminate use of those Scud missiles— nothing more than weapons of terror; . . . they can offer no military advantage, weapons of terror—it outraged the world what he has done.

Most military analysts agree that the ferocious air campaign was primarily responsible for the collapse of the Iraqi military after forty-three days of war. Daily press briefings from Central Command in Riyadh, Saudi Arabia, and from the Pentagon reported the number of Allied sorties flown daily and Allied casualties. They emphasized that the air war was being conducted solely against military targets. They repeatedly refused to estimate Iraqi deaths. On February 6, President Bush told a press briefing:

This [bombing campaign] has been fantastically accurate. And that's because a lot of money went into high technology weaponry—these laser-guided bombs and a lot of other things, Stealth technology. Many of these technologies, ridiculed in the past, now coming into their own and saving lives, not only American lives, Coalition lives, but the lives of Iraqis.

All of the gun camera videotapes released by the Pentagon during the war showed precision-guided bombs hitting military targets with breathtaking accuracy.

Air War Realities

It was only after the cease-fire that General Merrill A. McPeak, Air Force Chief of Staff, in a briefing on March 15, 1991, disclosed a more comprehensive and more truthful picture of the bombing campaign. By that account, a total of 88,500 tons of bombs were dropped in Iraq and occupied Kuwait. Of the total, only about 7 percent, or 6,520 tons, were precision-guided "smart" bombs, which hit their intended targets about 90 percent of the time. The other 93 percent were unguided "dumb" bombs. Of the 81,980 tons of unguided bombs, about 75 percent missed their targets, yielding an overall accuracy rate for the air war of about 30 percent.[1] On the accuracy of the gravity bombs raining down on Iraq from B–52s flying at thirty thousand feet, one retired admiral is reported to have said, "Most of them eventually hit the ground." The discrepancy between the purported accuracy of the air campaign and the reality of the campaign as it has emerged since war's end is particularly disturbing precisely because the moral rationalizations for U.S. conduct depended so heavily on those claims of precision.

But this was not the only troublesome issue raised by the air war. The war provided the first real opportunity to test a new generation of potent "conventional" weapons with near-nuclear explosive force, but without the radiation, fallout, and political revulsion of nuclear weapons. U.S. policy banned the use of nuclear weapons in the war (after Vice-president Quayle provocatively hinted that they might be used), but all the other new weapons were permitted. Most of them had been developed during the 1980s as alternatives to nuclear weapons for war in Europe against the Soviet Union. They included Multiple-Launch Rocket Systems, mobile containers that can launch twelve rockets up to twenty miles; Tomahawk sea-launched cruise missiles; Army Tactical Missile Systems, surface-to-surface missiles with a 20 mile range carrying about 950 explosive "bomblets"; the highly publicized laser-guided bombs; various types of cluster bomb units; and Standoff Land-Attack Missiles with 500-pound warheads fired from aircraft at distances beyond enemy air defenses.[2] "Penetration bombs," able to burrow through masses of earth and concrete before exploding, were used in the February 13 attack on an underground shelter in the Amariya section of Baghdad, which killed over three hundred civilians, mostly neighborhood residents. The incident set off an international controversy, as Pentagon officials first insisted that the building was a military command site and then conceded under pressure that their intelligence was not up-to-date. Occurring as it did during the Seventh Assembly of the World Council of Churches in Canberra, that shelter bombing was cited in the first paragraph of a comprehensive WCC policy statement on the Gulf War, lamenting "the mounting toll of victims on all sides, combatants and noncombatants alike, our own sisters and brothers."

Among the most lethal of the new weapons were the "fuel-air explosives," large bombs filled with a variety of highly volatile fuels. The fuels are released in a cloud over a large target area and then ignited, causing a fireball and pressure wave comparable to small nuclear weapons. They became the weapon of preference against dug-in and fortified troops.[3] Robert Scheer asks regarding these weapons: "And what about 'carpet bombing' troops senseless with fuel-air explosives that suck out the air and shake the earth with the power of a small nuclear explosion? In what way is this a moral act superior to using chemicals against troops?"[4] As other nations become enthralled by the high-tech dazzle of these weapons and scramble to develop their own, a new round of particularly dangerous "conventional" arms races is likely to result in the next years.

The One Hundred Hour Ground War

By all accounts, it was the six weeks of air bombardment that accounted for the brevity of the ground war, which lasted only four days. In fact, the campaign against Iraq, rather than a NATO-Warsaw Pact conflict in central Europe, at last provided the Pentagon with the first major test case of its much-touted, integrated "Air-Land Battle" strategy that had evolved during the last decade of the Cold War. The destruction of command-and-control centers by deep strategic bombing severely limited Iraqi intelligence and ground forces coordination. The relentless assault on supply lines left some Iraqi units without food and water. Demoralized troops whose equipment had been largely destroyed by air attacks and who had somehow survived carpet bombing found themselves exposed to what one U.S. officer called a "turkey shoot"; thousands of Iraqi "turkeys" were killed in those shoots. The devastation of bridges and other escape routes, the clogging of miles of highways, and the Coalition strategy of envelopment made retreat an impossibility for many divisions of Iraqi troops in Kuwait and southern Iraq. Surrender was a possibility only for some of these; slaughter was the fate of the others.

This stark contradiction between the most modern high-tech warfare and the primitivism of pitiless killing can only with the most tortuous ethical reasoning find justification in either the *jus in bello* principle of discrimination or the moral authority of the United Nations.

Destroying the Infrastructure

Pentagon leaders insisted throughout the war that, despite the occasional miss, their targeting policies were focused on Iraq's offensive military capacities. Destroying troops, fortifications, equipment, air defenses, supply lines, and command-and-control centers was to be the first order of business. Damage to civilian structures was consistently described as "collateral" and unintended. Such claims were the other

major theme (in addition to claims of precision) in
Pentagon assurances that it was conducting the war in
a highly moral fashion. Only after the cease-fire did a
more complete picture of U.S. and allied targeting
policies begin to emerge.

Daily "air-tasking" (targeting) orders were issued
by planning officers in the "Black Hole" Air Force
command headquarters in Riyadh under the overall
command of Lt. General Charles A. Horner. The
White House refrained from interfering in specific
targeting decisions. As Iraqi air defenses evaporated,
letting Allied planes attack unchallenged, the target
list in central Mesopotamia grew from about four
hundred to more than seven hundred. Railroads and
bridges, oil refineries, and most of Iraq's electric
plants were added to the list, primarily to increase the
impact of the war on Iraqi society and to increase Allied leverage over the Iraqi government after the
cease-fire.[5] Destruction of Iraq's electrical system was
particularly extensive. Before the war, Iraq had eight
steam generator sites, seven gas generator sites, and
five hydroelectric dams. At the cease-fire, only one
steam and one gas generator site remained undam-
aged. Destroying hydroelectric dams is forbidden under Protocol I, Article 56 of the Geneva protocols.

A team of Harvard public health experts visiting
Iraq in May 1991 reported that immediately after the
war Iraq generated only 4 percent of its prewar electricity output. By the May visit only 22 percent of output had been restored.[6] The Harvard team, the World
Health Organization, and UNICEF officials all expressed urgent concerns about the public health impact of the loss of water purification and supply,
refrigeration, sterilization, and sewage treatment and
disposal powered by electricity. Electricity is indis-
pensable for modern societies, and is particularly vul-
nerable because it cannot be stockpiled ahead of time.

One of the most morally convoluted statements in

the entire Gulf War came from a planning officer who commented:

> People say, "You didn't recognize that it was going to have an effect on water or sewage." Well, what were we trying to do with [United Nations-approved economic] sanctions—help out the Iraqi people? No. What we were doing with the attacks on infrastructure was to accelerate the effect of the sanctions.[7]

In other words, the nonviolent *alternative* international strategy of war was being "accelerated" by violent destruction.

Electrical facilities also were targeted because they could not be rebuilt quickly without technology imported from the West. Colonel John A. Warden III, deputy director of strategy, doctrine, and plans for the Air Force, explained:

> If there are political objectives that the U.N. coalition has, it can say, "Saddam, when you agree to do these things, we will allow people to come in and fix your electricity." It gives us long-term leverage.[8]

The destruction of railroads and bridges has compounded transport and public health problems. By some estimates, more people will die after the war from the destruction of the civilian infrastructure than died during the war itself. Robert Scheer laments:

> Tell me again why over a month of bombing, surgically or not, a civilian population doesn't qualify as terrorism. Come on, terrorizing the population was one of the prime goals of those tens of thousands of sorties; to turn the population of Iraq against Saddam. The goal might be noble but the means were the same as in hijacking a commercial aircraft, treating civilians as combatants.[9]

The Air Force decided not to bomb most of Iraq's crude oil-production facilities. But storage facilities, refineries, and pipelines were all destroyed, bringing to a halt all of Iraq's military and civilian gasoline-dependent transportation.

A United Nations report issued March 22, 1991, testified that Allied bombardment had thrown Iraq back to "the pre-industrial age." Iraq had been a substantially mechanized, electrified, twentieth-century society before the war. While most civilian homes and buildings may have been left standing at war's end, the life-support systems that sustained them were wiped out. Telephone exchanges and broadcast facilities were destroyed. Hospitals were largely incapacitated, resulting in death for many persons deprived of necessary equipment. Marti Ahtisaari, the U.N. Secretary-General's special envoy who prepared the U.N.'s postwar assessment, declared that "the Iraqi people may soon face a further imminent catastrophe, which could include epidemic and famine, if massive life-supporting needs are not rapidly met."[10] Later, that report became somewhat controversial, as other visitors assessed the war's impact more optimistically.

To be sure, Iraq also indulged in an infamous disregard for discrimination between civilians and the military. Iraq's Scud missile attacks against Israel and Saudi Arabia were intended to strike civilian areas. The atrocities wrought upon the people of Kuwait City were intended to destroy the fabric of that society, and the oil field fires were meant to devastate Kuwait's economy for years to come. Iraqi occupying forces rounded up thousands of civilian men in Kuwait and carted them off toward Iraq. These Iraqi atrocities and Saddam's bellicose rhetoric tended to reinforce the righteousness of U.S. claims of good conduct; they hardly excused the excesses of the air war.

Media, Censorship, and Propaganda

How was it possible for such a discrepancy to grow between American public perception of Allied war conduct and the reality of what Allied forces were doing? Much of the responsibility lies with what was, effectively, Pentagon censorship of the press during the Gulf War. Daily briefings broadcast live from Washington and Riyadh saturated the media with official versions of what was happening. Most members of the press covering the war in the region were excluded from participation in the small, select "pools"—and the pools were constantly accompanied by military personnel and unable to file their reports without prior military censorship. The Pentagon released video footage of the "smart" bombs in action, which was made-to-order for television's insatiable appetite for vivid pictures; such footage mesmerized press people as well as the rest of the country.

Ordinarily hard-nosed reporters were caught up in the tendentious jargon of the war and frequently forgot to ask hard questions; they practically became cheerleaders for the official line. Talk shows were dominated by retired military men enamored of the high-tech weapons. Critical or opposition voices were muted. A survey of the sources on the ABC, CBS, and NBC nightly newscasts conducted by Fairness and Accuracy in Reporting (FAIR) found that of 878 on-air sources, only one, Bill Monning of Physicians Against Nuclear War, was a representative of a national peace organization.[11] Another FAIR survey on the three nightly network news programs found that

> from the commitment of U.S. troops on Aug. 8 until Jan. 3, there was 2855 minutes of coverage of the crisis, but only 29 minutes that dealt with grassroots dissent, even though half the country opposed going to war.[12]

After the cease-fire, some mainline journalists did emerge as early critics of U.S. policy, as we noted in chapter 3.

The Pentagon's refusal to estimate Iraqi deaths was complemented by the media's own silence on the subject. On January 23, 1991, a day when weather conditions permitted some two thousand sorties over Iraq, Ted Koppel of ABC's "Nightline" reported, "Aside from the Scud missile that landed in Tel Aviv earlier, it's been a quiet night in the Middle East."

Media critic William F. Fore raises more fundamental questions about the American media's coverage of the Gulf War:

> The celebration of technology in the gulf war took place on stations increasingly owned and operated by multinationals deeply involved in the production of armaments. General Electric, the tenth largest corporation in the U.S. and one of the largest weapons producers, owns the NBC network and its stations. Westinghouse, another major defense contractor, owns one of the largest broadcast groups.[13]

GE aircraft engines were used in some twenty types of airplanes and helicopters used in the Gulf War. GE also manufactures parts for the Patriot missile. Fore continues:

> Sponsors also greatly influence the way news is presented. Dupont, IBM, AT&T, and ITT are all major sponsors on TV, and all have major stakes in the public support for high-tech armaments. Who benefits from coverage which celebrates smart bombs and surgical strikes?

> While it is true that television seeks out our psychological needs and meets them in ways that serve particular people's desires for money, power and control, it is also true that every person who views uncritically is asking to be controlled.[14]

The campaign to persuade the American public to believe that every effort was being taken to spare civilian lives and destruction, as well as to protect Coalition military personnel, was a resounding success for the Pentagon—and for the Bush administration. The reality behind the story, however, has proven quite different, tragically so for the people who were injured, have died, or will yet die from the conduct of the Gulf War.

9

Proportionality?
Truth About
the Consequences

The second *jus in bello* principle mandating just conduct in the waging of a war is that of *proportionality*. At the very least, proportionality requires that the harm wrought by a war must not be greater than the good it achieves. Yet the harm wrought by a war cannot be accurately estimated until some time after the war is over. Even then, the full extent of the harm can never be fully known. A discussion of proportionality rightly becomes an earnest effort to anticipate and understand the consequences, good and bad, of a war.

In his January 16 speech to the nation announcing the beginning of the air war, President Bush set forth his hopes for the good to be achieved:

> We have before us the opportunity to forge for ourselves and for future generations a new world order—a world where the rule of law, not the law of the jungle, governs the conduct of nations. . . . We have a real chance at this new world order, an order in which a credible United Nations can use its peacekeeping role to fulfill the promise and vision of the U.N.'s founders.

Days later, he told the Religious Broadcasters:

We all know that war never comes easy or cheap. War is never without tragedy. But when a war must be fought for the greater good, it is our gravest obligation to conduct a war in proportion to the threat. And that is why we must act reasonably, humanely, and make every effort possible to keep casualties to a minimum. And we've done so. I'm very proud of our military in achieving this end.

Appropriately enough, the president identified casualties as the first concern of proportionality. U.S. military strategy was designed to keep Allied casualties as low as possible and was conspicuously successful in doing so. *The Washington Post* reported a total of 304 U.S. dead, from combat and noncombat incidents, an extraordinarily small proportion of the 540,000 U.S. troops.

The Iraqi Death Toll

Iraqi casualties were much more difficult to count. The death toll, within thousands or even tens of thousands, may never be accurately known, partly because of mass burials in the desert sands and partly because of Iraqi secrecy. U.S. officials have repeatedly offered an estimate of 100,000 Iraqi soldiers killed, perhaps two-thirds or more as victims of the air campaign. In a substantial monograph on the Gulf War, Greenpeace summarized Iraq's losses as follows:

—100,000–120,000 military deaths
—5,000–15,000 civilian deaths during the war
—4,000–6,000 civilian deaths during March and April 1991 due to wounds, lack of medical care, or malnutrition
—20,000 Iraqis killed during the civil war in March
—15,000–30,000 Kurds and other refugees died on the roads or in camps.[1]

These estimates suggest that the total of military and civilian deaths in Iraq may have reached close to 200,000. The number of civilian deaths occurring after the war but attributable to its effects, whether civil strife or the devastation of life-support systems, was expected to rise for many months. The Harvard public health team estimated that in the coming year at least 170,000 more children would die of typhoid, cholera, malnutrition, and other health problems than would have died under normal conditions.

Shiite Uprising

On February 15 in Andover, Massachusetts, at a Raytheon Company plant that produces the Patriot missile, President Bush sent a message to groups within Iraq unhappy with Saddam Hussein's leadership:

> And there's another way for the bloodshed to stop, and that is for the Iraqi military and the Iraqi people to take matters into their own hands and force Saddam Hussein, the dictator, to step aside and then comply with the United Nations resolutions and rejoin the family of peace-loving nations.

Two large ethnic groups within Iraq responded to this call to overthrow Saddam: Kurds in the north and Shiites in the south. These two groups together represent nearly 80 percent of Iraq's population, but they have been unable to gather support from Saddam's power base, the Sunni elites of central Iraq.

Rebels contended that Bush's public statements were augmented by clandestine radio broadcasts from "The Voice of Free Iraq," which originated in Saudi Arabia. The broadcasts had used Kurdish and Islamic leaders to recruit their people for the rebellions and had at least implied promises of outside (U.S. and Saudi) help. When Bush refused to involve U.S.

forces in the rebellions, Kurdish leaders charged that the CIA had sponsored and financed the broadcasts and that the United States had a moral obligation to aid those who responded. CIA, State Department, and Pentagon officials all refused to confirm or deny U.S. participation in the broadcasts.[2] Whatever the truth with regard to the radio station itself, it is clear that the United States aroused expectations of support for the rebels that it was not prepared to implement, raising the question of moral complicity in the tragedies that followed.

Two days after the ceasefire, first reports began to trickle out that the southern Iraq city of Basra had rebelled against the authority of Saddam Hussein's government. The chaos was compounded by the influx of thousands of retreating Iraqi soldiers. Within days, fighting spread to at least twelve cities across southern Iraq, including Nassariyah, Jubayr, Kumayt, Najaf, and Karbala. Refugees began to stream into the U.S.-occupied zone in southern Iraq, reporting tortures and murders, tank battles and massive destruction. Refugees also fled to Iran and *into* Kuwait, in a tragically ironic reversal of fortune. A Western eyewitness cited evidence of food shipments and other logistical support from Iran for Shiite rebels.[3] A hard core of forty to fifty thousand Republican Guard troops loyal to Saddam moved quickly and brutally to suppress the rebellion. Basra and Karbala, revered by Shiites as home to the sacred mosques of al-Hussein and al-Abbas, suffered extensive damage, compounding that done by the Allied air war. Estimates of the death toll from the Shiite rebellion range from thirty thousand to a hundred thousand. "Everything is destroyed," a French relief worker reported after a visit to Karbala.[4] Months later, official Iraqi accounts of the southern revolt ascribed it primarily to at least three thousand armed "anarchists" who had infiltrated into Iraq from Iran with the goal of establishing a Shiite Islamic republic in the region. Diplomats confirmed that Iran did play a large role in the uprising. But long-simmering tensions between the Ba'ath party elites and the Shiite population of the south provided fertile ground for the uprising to take hold.[5] The southern cities have become armed camps. The wounds of those devastated cities will fester for years to come.

Kurds in Iraq

The tragic aftermath of the Gulf War for the Kurds is the latest chapter in a long and bitter history of conflict with Saddam Hussein's regime, its predecessors, and its neighbors. That history now includes at least two episodes of callous manipulation and mistreatment by the United States. Kurds have lived in the region that includes parts of Iran, Iraq, Syria, and Turkey since about 2400 B.C. Hopes for an autonomous Kurdistan emerged at the end of World War I, but were dashed by Kemal Ataturk of Turkey. In the early years of the Cold War, Kurdish aspirations were viewed by the United States as an opportunity for Soviet expansion in the region, and therefore were not supported.[6]

Still viewing the Kurds primarily through the lens of superpower competition, but as now on "our" side, in May 1972 President Nixon and National Security Adviser Henry Kissinger flew directly from the SALT I ceremony in Moscow to Tehran. There they arranged with the Shah to supply arms clandestinely to Kurdish rebels inside Iraq in order to destabilize Iraq as a Soviet client state and the Shah's archenemy.[7] During the next three years, at least $16 million of CIA money was sent to the Kurds to foment civil war, despite State Department opposition, and with no intention on the part of the administration that the Kurds should actually win. In January 1976 (when

George Bush was CIA director), the House Select
Committee on Intelligence Activities, chaired by
Congressman Otis Pike, firmly indicted the United
States in the ongoing tragedy of the Kurds:

> Documents in the Committee's possession clearly
> show that the President, Dr. Kissinger and the foreign
> head of state [the Shah] hoped that our clients [the
> Kurds] would not prevail. They preferred instead that
> the insurgents simply continue a level of hostilities suf-
> ficient to sap the resources of our ally's neighboring
> country [Iraq]. This policy was not imparted to our cli-
> ents [the Kurds], who were encouraged to continue
> fighting.[8]

Iran and Iraq reached agreement on March 15,
1975, in Algiers, trading Iraq's claim to the disputed
Shatt al-Arab waterway in return for Iran's sealing its
border to Kurdish insurgents. U.S. aid was withdrawn
abruptly from the Kurds, abandoning them to Iraq's
retribution and resettlement. Their leader, Mulla
Mustafa Barzani, fled to Iran and then to the United
States, where he died in 1979.

During the long years of the Iran-Iraq war, Kurds
were again caught in the middle, with both sides using
and abusing hostile Kurdish factions against the
other. In early 1987, before the war's end, Baghdad
unleashed draconian measures against Kurdish areas,
depopulating and razing villages and using chemical
weapons against civilians in Halabja and elsewhere.
Five days after the August 20, 1988, Iran-Iraq
ceasefire, Saddam Hussein launched a total assault
with sixty thousand troops and renewed gas attacks
on Kurdish nationalist positions. Within a week, sixty
thousand refugees were driven into Turkey and at
least that many more into Iran. The Kurdish national
army was decimated.[9]

On March 6, 1991, the day of President Bush's victory speech before a joint session of Congress,

Masoud Barzani, head of the Kurdish Democratic Party and a son of Mulla Mustafa Barzani, committed thousands of Pesh Merga troops, the Kurdish guerrilla army, to join the uprising. One week later Kurdish leaders claimed to control 75 percent of northern Iraq. After securing the Shiite south, Republican Guards rushed north to crush the Kurds with helicopter gunships, heavy artillery, and tanks. Within a week, the main military resistance was crushed. Half a million Kurdish civilian refugees fled along routes strafed by the helicopters to the mountains along the Iraqi-Turkish border, while perhaps a million struggled toward northern Iran. Cold, exposure, hunger, and disease struck particularly hard among the oldest and youngest refugees. Many had been injured by napalm and phosphorous bombs dropped by the Iraqi military. Turkey initially refused to allow Kurdish refugees to cross the border, although that position was later modified under international pressure.

Kurdish leaders once again charged their U.S. instigators with betrayal. Relief efforts were slow to arrive. During the first two months, more than 30 countries contributed $740 million in aid, of which $212 million came from the United States.[10] Eventually Allied forces established a security zone for Kurds along the Turkish border, which was guarded by U.S. troops until July 1991, when they were replaced by a small U.N. contingent. On April 24, Kurdish leaders announced an agreement in principle with Saddam Hussein to permit limited Kurdish autonomy and return of the refugees. But fear and suspicion remained dominant among the Kurds, and skirmishes with Iraqi troops resumed as the last U.S. soldiers withdrew.

The scale of the uprisings and the suffering they occasioned prompted a new debate in Washington. Some supporters, and some who originally opposed the war, suggested that perhaps the United States had ended the war too soon, leaving Saddam alive and

with too much military power intact. TV images of
the refugees' miseries dimmed the afterglow of the
"clean win," even as the official celebrations continued. These circumstances, along with renewed alarms
about Iraq's nuclear capabilities, led to proposals for
Gulf War II: a renewal of offensive military action
against Iraq.

Ecocatastrophes

Like the Vietnam War, the Gulf War was marked
by deliberate environmental devastation, in this case
by Iraq. The oil which so raised the stakes for the
Allies in defending Kuwait became the weapon that
fouled its land, air, and water. Iraqi forces occupying
Kuwait pursued two different oil-related ecological
strategies. Prior to January 15, they wired Kuwait's
oil fields and facilities with explosives. After the Coalition attack, they released oil directly into the Gulf
from Kuwaiti pipelines and storage tanks as well as
Iraqi tankers.

It has been impossible to make precise assessments
of the impact of the resulting oil slicks and smoke
clouds because of the vast scale of the damage, the
dangers in the war zone, the shortage of environmental scientists and equipment, and the secrecy and bi-
ases of the governments involved. An immediate
increase in respiratory diseases occurred in Kuwait itself. Summer's windlessness and blazing tempera-
tures compounded the health problems.

The environmental catastrophes spread far beyond
the borders of Kuwait and Iraq. Marine life in the
Gulf was severely affected. Much of Iran suffered
heavy air pollution, as did parts of Turkey, Bulgaria,
and the southern Soviet Union. Black snow was seen
in the Himalayas.[11] The enduring agricultural, marine, and public health consequences could only be
guessed. The extent to which long-term weather pat-

terns would be disrupted by the injection of smoke into the stratosphere is also unknown.[12]

The Bush administration blamed all the environmental damage on Iraq, whose behavior was incontestably reprehensible. Yet here, too, moral ambiguities remain. The United States and the Allies targeted Iraqi forces in Kuwait extensively during the bombing campaign. We do not know how many of the oil fires or pipeline leaks were, in fact, a result of Coalition bombing. But Coalition bombing of dams and other targets in Iraq clearly had serious environmental consequences. Moreover, Iraq began to use its environmental weapons only after George Bush launched his military offensive. As it became clearer that Iraq was losing and then that it would be routed in the ground war, the lighting of oil well fires accelerated dramatically.

The obvious bears recollection here. If the Gulf crisis had been overcome by a nonmilitary strategy, there might have been no sooty skies or oil slicks. If at the end a political settlement had at least prevented a ground war, much of the damage to air, soil, water, and health might not have been done.

The Peace Dividend: Another Casualty

After the wave of political revolutions across Eastern Europe in the fall of 1989 and the profound changes within the Soviet Union itself, a "peace dividend" seemed within range of a congressional consensus. Money released from high military budgets might at last be devoted to domestic programs or deficit reduction. Longtime proponents of "economic conversion" from military to civilian-based industry found themselves suddenly in popular demand. By the summer of 1990, both houses of Congress had passed military spending bills substantially lower than the administration's requested budget.

All that changed within days of Iraq's invasion of Kuwait. Almost immediately, the administration began to argue that the invasion had just shown that the Pentagon needed its entire budget request. In his speech of August 20 to the national convention of the Veterans of Foreign Wars, President Bush, although acknowledging deficit troubles, called for "a continued strong defense budget to support American troops":

> Make no mistake: to prevent aggression, to keep America militarily prepared, I will oppose the defense budget-slashers who are out of tune with what America needs to keep freedom secure and safe. . . . Most Americans . . . endorse giving the military the tools to do its job: The Peacekeeper [MX missile], the Midgetman, B–2 bomber and the Strategic Defense Initiative.

All the weapons mentioned on that short list were strategic nuclear weapons–related systems, designed as anti-Soviet weapons and completely unrelated to the eventual conduct of the Gulf War. But all were facing strong political resistance on Capitol Hill.

By fall both the rhetoric and the deployment in the Gulf were escalating, and all talk of the peace dividend had evaporated. The final, "compromise" military spending bill passed in the fall was substantially higher than either chamber had recommended during the summer, although still below the administration's request.

When the annual cycle of military spending legislation rolled around again in the spring of 1991, Congress had just been through the politically difficult January votes authorizing the Gulf War, and cries of "appeasement" and "soft on defense" were directed at those who had opposed the administration. The Gulf War was officially over. The extraordinary publicity it gave to Patriot missiles, cruise missiles and other smart weapons, F–117A stealth fighter aircraft, and M–1 tanks gave a new lease on life both to making more of those weapons and to many other marginally related weapons systems. Patriot successes showed we needed ballistic missile defense, the argument went, and that meant we needed strategic ballistic missile defense, and therefore the Strategic Defense Initiative (SDI, or "Star Wars"). In March, Senate Republicans floated a trial plan meant to directly abrogate the 1972 Anti-Ballistic Missile (ABM) Treaty, and on March 13 the House of Representatives defeated a similar proposal 145 to 281. In July, Senate Armed Services Committee leadership proposed the "Missile Defense Act of 1991," which would deploy a large ground-based missile defense system by the mid-1990s, costing tens of billions of dollars and that would likely violate the ABM treaty.

The military success of the F–117A stealth fighter (at $100 million per plane) allegedly showed that we needed the B–2 stealth bomber (at $865 million per plane), with both the Air Force and the Northrop Corporation (the B–2's manufacturer) emphasizing its possible use in conventional wars. Senators who had nearly succeeded in terminating the B–2 program in 1990 found the climate so changed in 1991 that they deferred even trying to do so in the spring. Although it was generally assumed that the administration's military budget request in 1990 (for fiscal year 1991) would be cut by Congress and the only question was by how much, in 1991 Congress approved the entire request without considering any efforts to cut it at all.

Long-range plans to close some military bases and to reduce the overall size of the United States armed forces are proceeding, driven by budget constraints. But hopes warmed by the end of the Cold War for deeper cuts in military spending, and for a comprehensive nuclear test ban, and for curbing the development of new weapons systems, and for reductions in

American workers' dependence on military contracts, have all been chilled. We cannot yet know how much these new facts of political life were goals of undertaking to fight the Gulf War and how much they are opportunistic consequences. All that is clear now is that they will have a long and fateful impact on the economic and social health of American society.

Domestic Policies and Politics

While the lost opportunity for a peace dividend diminished prospects for social, educational, health, and environmental programs, the U.S.-led Coalition victory over Iraq had a momentous impact on domestic politics, parties, and electoral prospects. George Bush's surging popularity as the victorious commander-in-chief appeared to assure his reelection in 1992 and to nullify the hopes of potential Democratic candidates. Professed affiliations with the Democratic Party dropped below Republican affiliations for the first time in decades. Liberal policies on civil rights, urban needs, health care, and abortion (including the social pronouncements of mainline churches) predictably faced years of frustration and defeat. Bush had clearly won the pot of "pure political gold" that John Sununu predicted would be the reward for a "short, successful war" against Iraq—at least for a while.

Consequences for the World's Poor

At Canberra in February 1991, a month after the United States initiated offensive military action against Iraq, the World Council of Churches Assembly called attention to "the global implications of the war" in these paragraphs:

> Among its chief victims have been the poor nations of the world, many of whom are already beset by internal conflicts and massive foreign debt.

Their peoples were among the first to suffer. Workers in the Middle East from countries like Sri Lanka, Bangladesh, the Philippines, India and Korea were either trapped in war zones or forced to flee under excruciating circumstances. The war has added to the drain on these nations' economies, some of which depended heavily on remittances from their nationals employed in the region which have now been cut off.

The war has dealt a massive economic blow to much of the developing world, eliminating major markets for primary exports, causing prices for fuels and petroleum products and for basic foodstuffs like rice and grain to skyrocket, and making the cost of other essential imports prohibitive for the poor.

The war has fanned the flames of religious, ethnic and regional conflicts in many countries, especially in Asia, seriously destabilizing some and giving rise to violent conflicts in others.

The preoccupation of the global mass media, governments, and international institutions with the war in the Gulf has distracted attention from efforts to resolve other armed conflicts raging around the world and from other present, massive human tragedies. It is estimated, for example, that some 20 million people are on the brink of starvation and death in the African countries of Sudan, Ethiopia, Somalia, Angola, Mozambique and Liberia. In this time of war, much of the world has turned a deaf ear to their cries for help.

A month later, a United Nations study provided extensive documentation for the World Council's concerns. The 42 poorest countries (with a per capita income of less than $200 a year) had already suffered deepening economic distress during the 1980s, due largely to collapsing commodity prices, mounting debt burdens, and massive joblessness. The Gulf War severely aggravated that distress, especially for countries whose citizens were guest workers in Iraq, Kuwait, and Saudi Arabia. Bangladesh lost $1.4 billion in wages, savings, and personal possessions. Yemen lost $1 billion in revenue and aid from Gulf countries. Sub-Sahara nations lost a similar amount due to increased oil and shipping costs.[13] There were no indications that the United States or other Coalition countries were prepared to assume major responsibility for alleviating such distress.

Summing Up the Consequences

In the anxious days of mid-January, just before the air war began, Senator Wyche Fowler of Georgia (a Presbyterian elder) reminded his Senate colleagues of Thucydides' account of the debates that preceded a famous Greek defeat in Sicily, and went on to say:

> The lesson is first and foremost the uncertainties of war, as true when the European powers plotted a brief, decisive war in 1914, as in 1964 when we sought no wider war in Vietnam, or in 415 B.C. when Athenians dreamed of glory on a far-off battlefield. In none of these cases did those who planned the conflict foresee the ultimate costs, in blood and treasure, of the long-range consequences of their action.[14]

Notwithstanding U.S.-Coalition success in forcing Iraq out of Kuwait, and doing so with minimal casualties on the offensive side, the ultimate costs and long-range consequences of the Gulf War are making the moral claims of proportionality more and more dubious. If George Bush and his aides can hardly be faulted for failing to anticipate all the war's costs and consequences, their continuing vaingloriousness about the war betrays a very limited range of moral sensitivity.

The enormity of Iraqi casualties and the unending suffering of the survivors, the environmental disasters, the lost peace dividend, the disdain for issues of domestic justice, the escalation of the arms trade, the seductive exhibitionism of high-tech weaponry, the deeper despair of the Palestinians, the aggravation of misery among the world's poorest peoples, and the implication of the United Nations in all these melancholy matters hardly add up to a vindication of, or by, the just war tradition.

10

Toward
a Just Peace

At the end of Operation Desert Storm on February 28, 1991, the chaos left by the war itself was immediately compounded by the eruption of civil strife within Iraq. To the casualties and wreckage of the war were added the rubble of more ruined cities which were largely spared by the war, along with more thousands of deaths and more than two million refugees and displaced persons.

Having authorized the war, the United Nations found itself at war's end burdened with myriad tasks of relief and security. Security Council Resolution 687 (April 9) decreed the terms of the cease-fire and established the U.N. Iraq-Kuwait Observer Mission (UNIKOM) to monitor a 15-kilometer-wide and 200-kilometer-long demilitarized zone between Iraq and Kuwait. UNIKOM's full complement included 1,400 troops from 36 countries (none from Middle Eastern states), under the command of an Austrian officer, Günther Greindl. The same resolution also created a Special Commission, chaired by Swedish diplomat Rolf Ekeus, to monitor the destruction of Iraq's nuclear, chemical, and biological weapon capabilities as well as its ballistic missiles.

Meanwhile, the U.N. Coordinator for Disaster Relief (UNDRO), the U.N. High Commissioner for Refugees (UNHCR), the U.N. Children's Fund (UNICEF), the World Health Organization (WHO), the World Food Programme (WFP), the Food and Agriculture Organization (FAO), and the U.N. Development Programme (UNDP) all deployed their strained resources throughout the region to aid in the work of relief and recovery.

Postwar Planning

Beyond these immediate but necessarily protracted tasks of postwar assistance, the even more daunting challenges of regional political and economic reconstruction confront the United Nations—and especially the United States. In March of 1991, shortly after the cease-fire in the Gulf, a Task Force on the Requirements of a Just Peace, established by the Washington-based Churches' Center for Theology and Public Policy, outlined a six-point agenda for "postwar planning for the Middle East and the world at large":

1. A comprehensive approach to Middle East conflicts, with resolute attention to the Israeli-Palestinian conflict and the legitimacy of Palestinian self-determination . . . and support of Security Council Resolutions 242 and 338 and "the principle of territory for peace."
2. A regional plan to curb the arms trade and eliminate weapons of mass destruction.
3. Multinational planning and cooperation for economic and environmental reconstruction and development, with urgent attention to overcom-

ing the extremes of poverty and wealth in the
Middle East.
4. Further development of multinational U.N.
   peacekeeping and security arrangements.
5. Instruments for the peaceful settlement of disputes, such as an arbitration panel to review
   Iraqi-Kuwaiti claims, renewed commitments to
   the World Court, and the good offices of the Secretary-General and other U.N. mediators.
6. Development of a cooperative and just world
   energy regime, based in part on a U.S. energy
   policy which stresses conservation and renew-
   able resources.[1]

On March 6, in his victory speech to a joint session
of Congress, President Bush addressed the first of
these points directly and vigorously, pledging support
of Resolutions 242 and 338 and adding this "guarantee": "No one will work harder for a stable peace in
the region than we will." Secretary of State Baker was
forthwith and repeatedly dispatched to Middle East
capitals for what proved to be exceedingly frustrating
rounds of shuttle diplomacy, preoccupied with the
table-setting arrangements of getting talks started
rather than with substantive issues. The Shamir government of Israel, while professing readiness for direct negotiations with Arab governments, remained
adamantly opposed to both U.N. and PLO participation in any comprehensive peace conference, and
gave no sign of compromise on the central controversies over territory and West Bank settlements. Israel's
tough bargaining position had clearly been fortified
by its military restraint during the Gulf War and also
by the PLO's disastrous embrace of Saddam Hussein.
Whether Israel had been rewarded with unpublicized
U.S. commitments concerning either the form or the
substance of peace negotiations may not be known for
a long time. In addition to presumptions of increased

economic assistance, there were unconfirmed reports of a U.S. promise not to push for Palestinian independence for a period of some years.

In a commencement address at the Air Force Academy on May 29, Bush outlined his approach to the second of these agenda items, arms control in the Middle East:

—A ban on the production and acquisition of nuclear weapons materials by all states in the region (but which would not require Israel to dismantle its own undeclared nuclear stockpile).

—The "eventual creation" of a nuclear-free zone in the region.

—A ban on the possession or use of chemical or biological weapons.

—An "ultimate" ban on surface-to-surface ballistic missiles.

—Discussions by the five major suppliers of conventional arms to the region (which just happen to be the five permanent members of the U.N. Security Council) to establish "guidelines for restraints on destabilizing transfers" of such arms. (In March, Bush had rejected Canadian Prime Minister Brian Mulroney's proposal for just such a meeting.)

Iran and Jordan immediately rejected the first of these proposals because it protected indefinitely Israel's nuclear arsenal.

The vagueness of the conventional arms proposal was criticized in Congress, where there has been strong support for an outright moratorium on the Middle East arms trade. Moreover, a White House statement could not even promise a reduction: Bush's "guidelines will permit states in the region to acquire the conventional capabilities they legitimately need to deter and defend against aggression." Casting further doubt on administration seriousness in curbing the arms trade, a report by the Arms Control Association disclosed that between August 2, 1990, and May 1991, the United States announced new arms deals amounting to $13.2 billion in the Middle East alone—and that total excluded "commercial sales" of an unknown amount by private U.S. contractors.[2] It is widely assumed that those private sales were largely made to Israel. Moreover, the administration projected $23 billion in arms transfers to the Middle East in fiscal year 1992 (out of a total of $33 billion worldwide).

As of mid-summer 1991, there had been little evidence of U.S. planning for the other long-range items on the agenda: economic justice in the Middle East, environmental reconstruction, permanent U.N. peacekeeping and security arrangements, instruments for peaceful settlement, a just world energy regime.

The United States and a New World Order

The trans-regional implications of peacemaking in the Middle East and the "new world order" rhetoric of the Gulf War do indeed provide a "defining moment" for Americans to decide what kind of world future we really want. Three extraordinarily productive and authoritative international commissions of the 1980s have helped greatly to focus the issues of the world's future. The reports of those three commissions, addressed to the United Nations and its member governments, point with particular force to American policies:

1. *The Independent Commission on International Development Issues,* chaired by Willy Brandt, former Chancellor of the Federal Republic of Germany. In an introduction to the commission's 1980 report, *North-South: A Program for Survival,* Brandt wrote that the primary concern of the commission was for peace. But he immediately added:

War is often thought of in terms of military conflict, or even annihilation. But there is a growing awareness that an equal danger might be chaos—as a result of mass hunger, economic disaster, environmental catastrophes, and terrorism. So we should not think only of reducing the traditional threats to peace, but also of the need for change from chaos to order.[3]

Brandt also frankly addressed some words to the United States and its leaders:

I do not believe that the American people could be indifferent to poverty and starvation anywhere in the world. . . . Yet the United States, which in the early 1960s was a leader in this field, has substantially reduced its international development efforts . . . to a very low level. . . . When the nations of the world join in an enterprise to enhance the chances of world survival and promote global prosperity, the most powerful and wealthy nation cannot be content to play a marginal role, and no one else would want it to.[4]

2. *The Independent Commission on Disarmament and Security Issues,* chaired by Olaf Palme, late Prime Minister of Sweden. The 1982 report of this commission, *Common Security: A Blueprint for Survival,* joined virtually all the critical military and disarmament issues that engaged the churches in the 1980s. In particular, the commission sought to displace the doctrine of nuclear deterrence by the concept of *common security:*

Security in the nuclear age means common security. Even ideological opponents and political rivals have a shared interest in survival. . . . A doctrine of common security must replace the present expedient of deterrence through armaments. International peace must rest on a commitment to joint survival rather than a threat of mutual destruction.[5]

In a prologue to the Palme Commission report, former Secretary of State Cyrus Vance (a commission member) wrote:

> The United States had a leading role in organizing the United Nations and in drafting its charter. Its goals reflect our ideals. Over the years, however, we . . . have drifted away from support for and use of the United Nations to contain and resolve conflicts which imperil regional and world peace. It is now past time for us to reverse that trend, to make a major effort to improve the way security problems are dealt with by the world organization.[6]

3. *The World Commission on Environment and Development,* chaired by Prime Minister Gro Harlem Brundtland of Norway. In a candid foreword to that commission's 1987 report, *Our Common Future,* Brundtland lamented:

> The present decade has been marked by a retreat from social concerns. Scientists bring to our attention urgent but complex problems bearing on our very survival: a warming globe, threats to the Earth's ozone layer, deserts consuming agricultural land. We respond by demanding more details, and by assigning the problems to institutions ill equipped to cope with them. Environmental degradation, first seen as mainly a problem of the rich nations and a side effect of industrial wealth, has become a survival issue for developing nations. It is part of the downward spiral of linked ecological and economic decline in which many of the poorest nations are trapped. . . . In the final analysis, this is what it amounts to: furthering the common understanding and common spirit of responsibility so clearly needed in a divided world.[7]

These three overarching global issues addressed by the independent commissions of the 1980s—economic equity, common security, environmental preservation—correspond felicitously to the great ecumenical study theme inaugurated by the 1983 Vancouver Assembly of the World Council of Churches: "Justice, Peace, and the Integrity of Creation." That theme continues to engage Christians on every continent in an ethical and theological quest for a more humane world community. It is a theme that suggests what a "new world order" could really be like, if we choose to make it so.

The moral and institutional imperatives highlighted by these three commissions were consolidated in April 1991 by a distinguished international working group known as The Stockholm Initiative on Global Security and Governance. Participants included Swedish Prime Minister Ingvar Carlsson, Willy Brandt, Gro Harlem Brundtland, Jimmy Carter, Václav Havel, Benazir Bhutto, Robert McNamara, Julius Nyerere, Eduard Shevardnadze, and Brian Urquhart. Released in the immediate wake of the Gulf War, the Stockholm Initiative's report, *Common Responsibility in the 1990s,* lamented the fact that the United Nations "was neither in a position to prevent the crisis, nor to solve it in a peaceful manner." Accordingly, the report advocated "improved United Nations capabilities for anticipating and preventing conflicts, in particular the establishment of a global emergency system." Recommendations for strengthening the United Nations' peacemaking and peacekeeping instruments were similar to those set forth more than two decades ago by the Commission to Study the Organization of Peace (outlined in chapter 3). A concluding proposal urges the calling of a World Summit on Global Governance, perhaps in 1995 on the fiftieth anniversary of the United Nations' birth at San Francisco. Preparations for such an event would be undertaken by an independent International Commission on Global Governance.[8]

Just War and Just Peace

At the outset of this case study, we suggested that the just war tradition offers a useful checklist of significant moral questions concerning both the resort to war and the actual conduct of war. The conspicuous citation of that tradition in public rhetoric during the Gulf conflict of 1990–91 persuaded us that the moral issues of the war could be illuminated, at least in part, by using the tradition's concepts as a framework for our analysis.

But we also indicated at the beginning that the fullness of justice is too often obscured, not only by the misuse and abuse of the just war tradition but by the limitations of the tradition itself.

A truly foundational ethic of war and peace must begin by taking the fullest possible account of the moral burdens of history that weigh upon any conflict between and among nations. Because historical responsibility for the causes of conflict typically is shared, a keen sense of the ambiguities of justice will help prepare conflicting nations for every prospect of peaceful settlement. Such a sense is spiritually nurtured especially by acknowledging the necessity of repentance as the precondition of reconciliation. The incapacity of nations and their leaders to admit even the possibility of repentance is often more a sign of weakness than of some real strength beneath their proud belligerence. That incapacity may also reflect profound historical ignorance or forgetfulness.

An adequate ethic of war and peace will not be totally preoccupied by the presumed evils of aggressive violence, whether border-crossings or insurrections. Too often the nations or groups perpetrating such acts have themselves been victimized by long histories of systemic violence in the form of economic exploitation, racial brutality, and political tyranny. Those who go to war against the victims of imperial and institutional oppression never have a monopoly on justice.

The justification of warfare and weaponry in terms of the traditional distinction between military and civilian targets has lost much of its presumed clarity. Modern military technology is produced by intricate complexes of government bureaucracies, arms industries, research institutions, power plants, and communications and transportation systems: complexes that intimately mesh military activities with most other social institutions, even with basic infrastructures. From a strategic perspective, therefore, it may seem necessary for bombs and missiles to attack an unlimited range of targets throughout a society's institutional fabric. But the direct and indirect civilian casualties and devastation from such warfare (as was the case in U.S.-Coalition warfare against Iraq) make invocations of the traditional norms of just conduct increasingly fatuous.

The traditional preoccupation with an *ethic of intention* to distinguish between military and civilian targets must yield to a much more consequential ethic that knows how indiscriminately destructive and deadly warfare has become—an *ethic that therefore strengthens the presumption against any resort to war.* The "collateral damage" done by either conventional or unconventional weapons can scarcely be justified any longer by the traditional claim of "double effect," that is, that such "damage" is the unintended consequence of military action. No consequence of the Gulf War is more dangerous or more perverse than the pretentious assumption that the presumed "success" and "morality" of the U.S.-Coalition assault on Iraq have, once again, made the resort to war an acceptable option or even a paradigm for the future of military policy.

The possession of overwhelming military force by a great power makes genuinely multilateral institutions of peacemaking and peacekeeping more important, not less so, lest the great power presume police authority to intervene in conflicts anywhere in the world. Multilateral institutions acting within a framework of common security potentially offer more effective instruments for crisis intervention, war prevention, and military restraint than the "might makes right" presumptions of a great power.

What is particularly perilous—witness the Gulf War—is a great power's pressuring an international organization for a global license to decide unilaterally whether, when, how, and to what extremes to wage war. The moral pretenses to universalism by a great power can be among the most demonic forces of history. Essentially unilateral warfare tends, much more than do international organizations, to make use of hate images, untruthful propaganda, and spurious appeals to patriotism—all of which intensify hostilities and make peaceful settlement especially difficult.

Another particularly grievous legacy of the Gulf crisis is the unilateral U.S. decision to abandon primary reliance on economic sanctions. Those sanctions offered one of history's most promising opportunities to demonstrate the viability of a nonmilitary strategy of crisis intervention. Although the U.N. Security Council had approved the sanctions, the council was never given the opportunity to decide whether or when or how to wage the war conducted in its name. The near-universal condemnation of Iraq's aggression and of support for sanctions was badly eroded by the Bush administration's own aggressive use of "all necessary means." The authorization of "all necessary means" had been promoted, to both the United Nations and Congress, as strengthening Bush's hand to obtain a peaceful settlement—but, whether through intention or impatience, nonmilitary means were never given a fair trial.

The just war tradition best serves the imperatives

of peacemaking in teaching us that justice is not, first and foremost, a call to arms, to violence and vengeance. In the principle of last resort, the tradition stringently commands peaceful settlement as first resort and as persistent resort. Harold Saunders, former Assistant Secretary of State for Near Eastern Affairs, wrote after the U.S. air assault on Iraq began:

> Learning to work effectively in our changing world requires us not just to give lip service to the old notion that war is a last resort. We have to devote all creative energy to imagining new ways of producing results by political means, since military action is becoming intolerably costly.
>
> When the first bomb dropped in the war to roll back Iraqi aggression, the hope of using the Gulf crisis of 1990–91 to establish a new world order was seriously undercut.
>
> The practical question is whether and how policymakers can devise ways of confronting lawless and evil acts effectively by using instruments that will not destroy what they are trying to preserve.
>
> For many who are also concerned with the ethics of policy, a political approach offers the possibility of actions not based mainly on firepower but on the power that emerges from political relationships built on mutual consent and shared purposes.[9]

In the biblical story, the understanding of justice arises from the primitive notion of unlimited revenge and moves to proportional retaliation, to the renunciation of vengeance, to the disclaiming of ultimate judgment on the sins of others, to the faithful conviction that *justice is lovingkindness,* for justice is grounded in the love and mercy of God. That affirmation does not settle the old debates between pacifists and just-war advocates, but it does command an ethic of justice that is indivisible from peacemaking. In the *shalom* of God and God's good creation, justice and peace do not contradict each other: they are one.

Such an ethic will nerve the creation of trans-national institutions of community and common security in which all nations, the most powerful and the least powerful, are alike subject to the sanctions of equity and of law. And it will nurture the ways of both peaceful change and peaceful settlement, because even for the most justifiable of just causes, war has truly become a last, last resort—and will even then most likely be a terrible injustice and an immeasurably tragic blunder.

Notes

Chapter 1. Ethics and Desert Storm

1. John Howard Yoder, "Just War Tradition: Is It Credible?" *The Christian Century* (March 12, 1991), 295–298. Yoder's article was a response to a debate on the Gulf War in the February 6–13, 1991, issue of *The Christian Century:* James Turner Johnson, "The Use of Force: A Justified Response," and Alan Geyer, "Just War and the Burdens of History," pp. 134–135. See also Alan Geyer, "Just War, Jihad, and Abuse of Tradition," *Christianity and Crisis* (March 4, 1991), 51–53.

Chapter 2. Just Cause? The Roots of Conflict

1. Arthur Balfour, quoted in Christopher Sykes, *Crossroads to Israel* (London: Collins, 1965), 13.

2. Glenn Frankel, "Imperialist Legacy: Lines in the Sand," *The Washington Post* (August 31, 1990), A20.

3. *Ibid.*

4. Walter Pincus, "Kuwait Crisis Foreshadowed by '61 Affair," *The Washington Post* (April 2, 1991), A16.

5. Frankel, "Imperialist Legacy."

6. John K. Cooley, "Pre-War Gulf Diplomacy," *Survival* (March/April, 1991), 25.

7. *Ibid.,* 22.

8. *Ibid.,* 25.

9. *Ibid.,* 24.

Chapter 3. Just Cause? Questions of Complicity

1. "A Man You Could Do Business With," *Time* (March 11, 1991), 59.

2. "Avoiding the Next Crisis," *Newsweek* (March 11, 1991), 58.

3. Don Oberdorfer, "Mixed Signals in the Middle East," *The Washington Post Magazine* (March 17, 1991), 20.

4. A detailed account of the anti-Mossadegh coup is provided in David Wise and Thomas B. Ross, *The Invisible Government* (New York: Random House, 1964), 110–114. See also Paul W. Blackstock, *The Strategy of Subversion* (Chicago: Quadrangle Books, 1964), 226.

5. William G. Carleton, *The Revolution in American Foreign Policy* (New York: Random House, 1963), 82.

6. "A Man You Could Do Business With," 59.

7. *Ibid.,* 61.

8. See also Michael T. Klare, "Fueling the Fire: How We Armed the Middle East," *Bulletin of Atomic Scientists* (January–February 1991), 19–26.

9. Joe Conason, "The Iraq Lobby: Kissinger, The Business Forum & Co.," *The New Republic* (October 1, 1990), 15.

10. William B. Quandt, ed., *The Middle East: Ten Years After Camp David* (Washington, D.C.: The Brookings Institution, 1988), 15.

11. *Ibid.,* 360.

12. William B. Quandt, "The Middle East in 1990," *America and the World 1990/91, Foreign Affairs* (January 1991), 56.

13. *The United Nations: The Next Twenty-five Years* (New York: Commission to Study the Organization of Peace, 1969), 32–33.

Chapter 4. Just Intent? War Aims in the Gulf

1. *Pressing for Peace: The Churches Act in the Gulf Crisis* (New York: National Council of Churches, January 1991), 3.

2. *Ibid.,* 8.

3. Arthur Schlesinger, Jr., *The Wall Street Journal* (January 7, 1991), A14.

4. Elizabeth Drew, "Letter from Washington," *The New Yorker* (February 4, 1991), 82.

5. Bob Woodward, *The Commanders* (New York: Simon & Schuster, 1991), 259–260.

6. Don Oberdorfer, "Bush's Talk of a 'New World Order': Foreign Policy Tool or Mere Slogan?" *The Washington Post* (May 26, 1991), A31.

7. Stephen J. Solarz, "The Stakes in the Gulf," *The New Republic* (January 7–14, 1991), 21.

8. Henry A. Kissinger, "A False Dream," in Micah L. Sifry and Christopher Cerf, eds., *The Gulf War Reader* (New York: Times Books, Random House, 1991), 461.

9. Jim Wallis, "A Neither Just Nor Holy War: Dissenting from the New World Order," *Sojourners* (April 1991), 12.

10. Thomas L. Friedman, "Confrontation in the Gulf: U.S. Gulf Policy—Vague 'Vital Interest,' " *The New York Times* (August 12, 1990), 1.

11. Christopher Hitchens, "Realpolitik in the Gulf: A Game Gone Tilt," *Harper's* (January 1991), 71–72.

12. Lewis H. Lapham, "Onward Christian Soldiers," in Sifry and Cerf, pp. 452–453.

13. "A Neither Just nor Holy War," 12.

14. Nubar Hovsepian, "New World Order: Destroying Arab Society?" *Christianity and Crisis* (February 18, 1991), 27–28.

15. Joe Stork and Martha Wenger, "From Rapid Deployment to Massive Deployment," in Sifry and Cerf, 36.

16. Michael Klare, "The Pentagon's New Paradigm," in Sifry and Cerf, 466–475.

17. Caspar Weinberger, quoted in Stork and Wenger, 37.

18. Friedman, "Confrontation in the Gulf," 1.

19. Charles William Maynes, "Dateline Washington: A Necessary War?" *Foreign Policy* (Spring 1991), 159–170.

20. James M. Wall, "Hussein's Designs, Bush's Intentions," *The Christian Century* (March 6, 1991), 251–252.

21. Woodward, *The Commanders,* 89.

22. *Ibid.,* 260–261.

23. *Ibid.,* 85.

24. *Ibid.,* 91.

25. *Ibid.,* 81.

26. Drew, "Letter from Washington," 183.

27. *Ibid.,* 182.

Chapter 5. Last Resort? The Miles of Peace

1. Elizabeth Drew, "Letter from Washington," *The New Yorker* (February 4, 1991), 82.

2. *Ibid.,* 185–186.

3. Jimmy Carter, "The Need to Negotiate," *Time* (October 22, 1990), 43.

4. Bob Woodward, *The Commanders* (New York: Simon & Schuster, 1991), 337.

5. John K. Cooley, "Pre-War Gulf Diplomacy," *Survival* (March/April 1991), 129.

6. Woodward, *The Commanders,* 237.

7. Stanley Reed, "Jordan and the Gulf Crisis," *Foreign Affairs* (Winter 1990/91), 22.

8. Cooley, "Pre-War Gulf Diplomacy," 131–132.

9. *Ibid.,* 134.

10. *Ibid.,* 134–135.

11. *Ibid.,* 137.

12. Drew, "Letter from Washington," 85.

13. "United Nations: The End Game," *Middle East International* (22 February 1991), 6.

14. Javier Pérez de Cuéllar, *International Document Review,* vol. 2, no. 13 (April 1991), 15–19.

15. Yevgeni Primakov, "My Final Visit with Saddam Hussein," *Time* (March 11, 1991), 45.

Chapter 6. Legitimate Authority? War Powers in Desert Storm

1. Fred Strasser, "Gulf War May Have Blazed a Trail for International Law," *The Christian Science Monitor* (March 21, 1991), 19.

2. *Ibid.*

3. Lawrence D. Weiler, *A Memo on U.S. Policy and U.N. Authority* (Washington: The Churches' Center for Theology and Public Policy, March 1991).

4. Bob Woodward, *The Commanders* (New York: Simon & Schuster, 1991), 333–335.

5. Lee Hamilton, "Who Voted 'Wrong'?" *The Washington Post* (March 10, 1991), D7.

6. *Pressing for Peace: The Churches Act in the Gulf Crisis* (New York: National Council of Churches, January 1991), 8–9.

7. Noam Chomsky, "The Use (and Abuse) of the United Nations," in Micah L. Sifry and Christopher Cerf, eds., *The Gulf War Reader* (New York: Times Books, Random House, 1991), 308–309.

8. Richard H. Ullman, "Paths to Reconciliation: The United States in the International System of the Late 1980s," in Sanford J. Ungar, ed., *Estrangement: America and the World* (New York: Oxford University Press, 1985), 283.

9. Woodward, *The Commanders,* 338.

10. *Ibid.,* 356–357.

11. Lee Hamilton, "Who Voted 'Wrong'?"

Chapter 7. Prospect of Success? Expectations of Victory

1. "Fact Sheet: The Gulf Coalition," Arms Control and Foreign Policy Caucus, U.S. Congress, January 10, 1991.

2. "Facing Off: The Balance of Forces," *The Washington Post* (January 15, 1991), A15.

3. "U.S. Invasion of Iraq: Appraising the Option," *The Defense Monitor,* vol. XIX, no. 8 (1990), 3.

4. "Iraq Fortifies Kuwait, Awaits U.S.," *San Francisco Examiner* (November 1, 1990), A15.

5. Steve McCurry, "In the Eye of Desert Storm," *National Geographic* (August 1991), 34.

6. Lewis H. Lapham, "Brave New World," *Harper's* (March 1991), 14.

Chapter 8. Discrimination? Scrupulous Conduct in War

1. Barton Gellman, "U.S. Bombs Missed 70% of Time," *The Washington Post* (March 16, 1991), A1.

2. Michael T. Klare, "High-Death Weapons of the Gulf War," *The Nation* (June 3, 1991), front cover, 738–742.

3. *Ibid.*

4. Robert Scheer, "What a Wonderful War," in Micah L. Sifry and Christopher Cerf, eds., *The Gulf War Reader* (New York: Times Books, Random House, 1991), 494.

5. Barton Gellman, "Allied Air War Struck Broadly in Iraq," *The Washington Post* (June 23, 1991), A1, A16.

6. *Ibid.*

7. *Ibid.*

8. *Ibid.*

9. Scheer, "What a Wonderful War," in Sifry and Cerf, 494.

10. "Kurds, Iraqi Forces Are Reported Waging Heavy Fighting in North," *The Washington Post* (March 22, 1991), A20.

11. Jim Naureckas, "Gulf War Coverage: The Worst Censorship Was at Home," *Extra!,* vol. 4, no. 3 (May 1991), 5.

12. "Anti-Anti-War Coverage = Pro-War Coverage," *Extra!,* 19.

13. William F. Fore, "Analyzing the Military-News Complex," *The Christian Century* (April 17, 1991), 422–423.

14. *Ibid.*

Chapter 9. Proportionality? Truth About the Consequences

1. William M. Arkin, Damian Durrant, and Marianne Cherni, *On Impact: Modern Warfare and the Environment. A Case Study of the Gulf War* (Washington: Greenpeace, 1991), 15.

2. Barton Gellman, "Kurds Contend U.S. Encouraged Rebellion Via 'Voice of Free Iraq,' " *The Washington Post* (April 9, 1991), A17.

3. "Pro-Saddam Forces Appear to Be Putting Down Iraqi Rebellion in South," *The Washington Post* (March 7, 1991), A34.

4. Glenn Frankel, "Iraq: Despotism Amid the Ruins," *The Washington Post* (April 9, 1991), A17.

5. Caryle Murphy, "Iraqi Holy Cities Become Armed Camps," *The Washington Post* (June 30, 1991), A1, A23.

6. William Linn Westermann, "Kurdish Independence," *Foreign Affairs,* 1946, reprinted in *Foreign Affairs,* Summer 1991, 50–54.

7. Seymour M. Hersh, *The Price of Power: Kissinger in the Nixon White House* (New York: Summit Books, 1983), 542n.

8. Quoted in Christopher Hitchens, "Realpolitik in the Gulf: A Game Gone Tilt," *Harper's* (January 1991), 71.

9. David McDowall, *The Kurds* (The Minority Rights Group Report No. 23; London: 1985, 1989), 27. See also Melissa J. Gillis, "The Kurds: A History of Suffering" (New York: Presbyterian United Nations Office, 1991).

10. "Two-Month Iraqi Refugee Death Toll Set at 6,700," *The Washington Post* (June 8, 1991), A16. The statistic refers to Turkish border camps only.

11. "Kuwait's Oily Nightmare Slowly Abates," *The Washington Post* (June 8, 1991), A16.

12. William Arkin et al., *On Impact,* p. 69. See also Thomas Y. Canby, "After the Storm," *National Geographic* (August 1991), 2–33.

13. William Drozdiak, "World's Poorest Nations Hit Hard by Gulf Crisis, U.N. Says," *The Washington Post* (March 21, 1991), A23.

14. Wyche Fowler, quoted in R. W. Apple, Jr., "Prophets of War," *The New York Times* (January 13, 1991), section 4, 1.

Chapter 10. Toward a Just Peace

1. *A Statement on the Middle East and a Just Peace* (Washington: The Churches' Center for Theology and Public Policy, March 1991), 3–4.

2. "U.S. Arms Transfers to the Middle East Since August 2, 1990," *Arms Control Today* (June 1991), 26.

3. The Independent Commission on International Development Issues, *North-South: A Program for Survival* (Cambridge: MIT Press, 1980), 13.

4. *Ibid.,* 27.

5. The Independent Commission on Disarmament and Security Issues, *Common Security: A Blueprint for Survival* (New York: Simon & Schuster, 1982), 139.

6. *Ibid.,* x.

7. The World Commission on Environment and Development, *Our Common Future* (New York: Oxford University Press, 1987), xi–xv.

8. The Stockholm Institute on Global Security and Governance, *Common Responsibility in the 1990s* (Stockholm: Prime Minister's Office, 1991), 5, 12–13, 41.

9. Harold H. Saunders, "Political Settlement and the Gulf Crisis," *Mediterranean Quarterly* (Spring 1991), 5, 6, 16.

Index

DATE DUE

CENTER FOR PEACE LEARNING
GEORGE FOX COLLEGE
NEWBERG OR, 97132